D1503539

THE FIELD *of* IMAGINATION

THE FIELD
of
IMAGINATION

Thomas Paine and
Eighteenth-Century Poetry

SCOTT M. CLEARY

University of Virginia Press
Charlottesville and London

University of Virginia Press
© 2019 by the Rector and Visitors of the University of Virginia
All rights reserved
Printed in the United States of America on acid-free paper

First published 2019

1 3 5 7 9 8 6 4 2

Library of Congress Cataloging-in-Publication Data
Names: Cleary, Scott, author.
Title: The field of imagination : Thomas Paine and eighteenth-century poetry /
Scott M. Cleary.
Description: Charlottesville : University of Virginia Press, 2019. |
Includes bibliographical references and index.
Identifiers: LCCN 2019016150 | ISBN 9780813942933 (cloth : alk. paper) |
ISBN 9780813942940 (e-book)
Subjects: LCSH: Paine, Thomas, 1737–1809—Criticism and interpretation. |
Paine, Thomas, 1737–1809—Literary style. | Paine, Thomas, 1737–1809—
Influence. | American poetry—18th century—History and criticism. | Political
poetry, American—History and criticism. | Epigraphs (Literature) | Poets,
American—Biography. | Revolutionaries—United States—Biography.
Classification: LCC PS819 .C58 2019 | DDC 811/.2—dc23
LC record available at https://lccn.loc.gov/2019016150

Cover art: "Citizen Don Quixote Becomes the Champion of French Principles,"
James Sayers, 1794 (TPNHA Collection at Iona College);
parchment background (iStock/SonerCdem)

To Tonia

"Most sincerely do I wish you all the good
that heaven can bless you with."

—*Letter to Kitty Nicholson Few, January 6, 1789*

To Lucan

"If there must be trouble, let it be in my day,
that my child may have peace."

—*Crisis I*, December 23, 1776

Just then Tom Paine, himself
Came running from across the field

—Bob Dylan, "As I Went Out One Morning"

Contents

Acknowledgments

My personal thanks go to the staffs of the Monmouth County Histori-cal Association, the New York Public Library, the American Philosophical Society, the New York Historical Society, the Houghton Library, Harvard University, and the Ryan Library, Iona College, for their help with the dias-pora of Paine's archival material and that of those he influenced. Gary Ber-ton and the Thomas Paine National Historical Association were constant sources of information and aid. Long may they promote the life, legacy, and works of Paine.

Family in all its forms were vital to the writing of this book. Mike and Maria Cristofaro; Joey, Michelle, and Michelle Londyn Cristofaro; and Brian, Francesca, and Jake Williams: thank you for your support. My par-ents, Michael and Patricia Cleary, taught me a love of literature and toler-ance of politics that was temperamentally perfect for the issue of Paine and poetry. And last to Tonia and Lucan Cleary, to whom this book is dedicated. This could not and would not have been written without you.

Portions of this book were previously published in "Thomas Paine and Po-etic Liberty," *Enlightenment Liberties/Libértes des Lumières: Actes du séminaire de la Société internationale d'étude du XVIIe siècle,* edited by Guillaume An-sart, Raphael Ehrsam, Catriona Seth, and Yasmin Solomonescu (Éditions Honoré Champion, Paris: 2018), 305–18.

THE FIELD *of* IMAGINATION

Introduction

In the year of America's birth, in the coldest of months, a small band of patriots huddled by dying campfires on the shores of an icy river. The capital was abandoned. The enemy was advancing. The snow was stained with blood. At the moment when the outcome of our revolution was most in doubt, the father of our nation ordered these words to be read to the people: "Let it be told to the future world . . . that in the depth of winter, when nothing but hope and virtue could survive . . . that the city and the country, alarmed at one common danger, came forth to meet it."

—President Barack Obama, inaugural address, January 20, 2009

History has always found a way of embroiling Thomas Paine in moments of both American and global significance. On a chilly January Tuesday in 2009, Barack Obama was inaugurated as the first African American president in the history of the republic, a long-awaited and necessary fulfillment of the most tantalizing promises the Declaration of Independence proclaimed two centuries prior. Toward the end of his inaugural speech, President Obama recited the words above, invoking the first father of the nation and his attempts to rally colonial troops. But in quoting George Washington, President Obama elided Thomas Paine; in seeking to connect his own nascent presidency with the first, President Obama neglected to mention whose words Washington ordered to be read to the people: Thomas Paine's, from his first *Crisis* paper. Paine's words were present; Paine's presence was absent. The putative founding father whose body was famously disinterred and whose bones were lost to history provided one of the culminating statements to a unique moment in American political history, but could not be named in deference to Washington, a man who Paine, in his *Letter to George Washington* (1797), accused of having "this cold hermaphrodite faculty that imposed itself upon the world, and was credited for a while." This study of Paine and eighteenth-century poetry is an attempt to credit Paine for a while—to examine how Paine, as much through his poetry as his better-known pamphlets and essays, fashioned for himself a distinctive role in the emergence of a transatlantic print culture and strategically manipulated his available literary contexts as he wrote, borrowed, adapted, and was represented in poetry both British and American.

Indeed, I would suggest that Paine is an interesting person to consider in the cleavage between those two cultural and national poetic markers. As Leonard Tennehouse has written, "After the War of Independence, there is every reason to believe that citizens of the United States knew—and felt keenly—that they were no longer subjects of Great Britain. But it does not necessarily follow from this that the colonists renounced their English identity."[1] And if poetry is one of those aspects of English identity, then Paine complicates such knowing and feeling because he was an early and passionate advocate for constructing an American identity on what he saw as the ruins, not continuation, of a British one. That is why early American poets like Philip Freneau and Joel Barlow looked to him as a poetic figure and inspiration. It is likewise why British poets in the 1790s saw Paine as an existential threat to their existence as Englishmen, and why Paine himself epigraphically drew on two famed, contentious British poets to make specifically American claims on American issues during the War of Independence. He was utterly unperturbed by what it might mean for a colonial American to be British. While drawing on the British issues they addressed, he was not drawing on those British poets for their Britishness, but for their poetic contributions to his own political ideas as he was trying to forge American identity through his writings.

To insist that poetry be considered part of those writings reflects, but also offers a solution to, what Mark Philp has characterized as a "problem in knowing how to approach the diverse writings and activities of the writer and polemicist" and "think[ing] of someone's oeuvre as a consistent and coherent, interrelated whole."[2] For Philp, that problem is specifically political, but Paine's poetry suggests that a loose coalition of practices conventionally called print culture is one way to frame, and thus solve, that problem, inasmuch as the term print culture itself is not unproblematized. As James Raven has noted, the term "threatens to isolate . . . a broader cultural history in which the relationship between text and audience was often influenced by other modes of social interaction."[3] Paine's commerce with various expressions of eighteenth-century poetry is one way to recover and reintegrate that cultural history in order to delineate his literary contexts and observe how he embraced and shaped print culture whenever it suited both his political and poetic ends. More than his well-known pamphlets and political works, poetry became a privileged modality of print culture negotiation for Paine, a form of literary expression into which he could embed his chosen suite of print culture practices and through which he could mold the social dynamics at the heart of his political claims. In his own early poetry, Paine considers those social formations as essential to both the American literary marketplace and the identity arising from it. In his epigraphic borrowing of popular and charismatic British poets, he renders such social interaction as a valve to transatlantic circulation, concerned with how their British ideas explained and justified his own American arguments. In his manuscript poetry, Paine tacitly acknowledges and exploits fissures in the hegemonic ascendancy of print culture by the century's end, and in the poetry of early America's two foremost poets, Paine himself is an embedded constituent of print culture practices. For Philip Freneau it is because Paine was an exemplary practitioner of those practices; for Joel Barlow it is because he was an exemplary theorist of them and their political consequences. Whether in print or manuscript, and as British or American, poetic figure or poetic influence, editor or poet, Paine is fascinatingly multi-faceted and essential to consider in the workings of transatlantic eighteenth-century poetry, and poetry itself is as important as his political works in considering Paine's impact on the late eighteenth-century age of political revolutions and their socioliterary contexts.

My first chapter explores Paine's earliest American experience, his editing of the *Pennsylvania Magazine* in the thriving literary marketplace of colonial Philadelphia, where Paine could both trend and trend set. For its first six issues, from January to July of 1775, Paine's contributions and editorial control gave him a print vehicle through which he could explore, test, and cultivate his political ideas concerning the possibility of independence as a viable if still somewhat controversial idea. My contention is that the poetical essays included in every issue, some of the magazine's most critically neglected aspects, were the privileged literary spaces and print culture modalities in which Paine as editor could fulfill two crucial functions: to include the poetry—his own and others—that served his own political views, and to build intertextual meanings and connections between and amongst pieces in the magazine. What emerges is an editorial tenure in which Paine shaped the magazine's poetry to serve his political aspirations in ways the magazine's prose could not.

My second chapter looks at the two poems Paine first published in the *Pennsylvania Magazine* and on which Paine himself hinged his poetic reputation: "Liberty Tree" and "The Death of General Wolfe." The first leverages political reform through the burgeoning social formulations and networks that were developing in America. Essential to this poetic program is Paine's delightfully subversive borrowing of the tropes of British liberty and the poems written to support it. The second, despite its apparent celebration of James Wolfe, the British hero of Québec, is an early indicator of Paine's disquiet with British claims to liberty, in part because it differs from the virtual subculture of Wolfe poetry that emerged in the eighteenth century. It also reflects his early participation in clubs and societies, and the social configurations that would shape his own political views and arguments for American independence. Demonstrating an early acquaintance with poetic conventions and mythology, the poem was an ideal vehicle for a young man finding his poetic and political footing amidst cries of "Wilkes and Liberty" and the calls for political reform that would echo a decade later in the revolution.

No work inspired that revolution more than Paine's *Common Sense*. The most mythologized of his texts, and the one staking Paine's claim as a quasi-member of the founding fathers, its critical heritage has singularly failed to seriously consider a poetic choice Paine made plain for his readers to see: a quotation from the British poet James Thomson on the title page. Paine's choice of quotation comes from Thomson's "Liberty," a less popular work than his *Seasons*, in which Thomson makes arguments for Whig ascendency and the perpetual but highly problematized dominance of British Liberty as a native virtue. This deconstructive impulse offers a provocative epigraphic context for *Common Sense* in its calls for separation from Britain, and my third chapter endeavors to demonstrate the degree to which Paine is indebted to Thomson for both the structure and content of his most famous pamphlet.

Thomson, though, is not the only British poet to influence Paine, as my fourth chapter shows. Paine's *Crisis* papers, the place of which in American myth was exemplified by President Obama's quotation, serve as one of the premier chronicles of the revolution, starting in late 1776 and ending in 1783. Numbering sixteen in total, the papers have only a single poetic epigraph among them: a couplet in the second *Crisis* paper taken from Charles Churchill, the provocative, nihilistic British poet whose poetic and periodical contentions against the reign of George III and the ministry of John Stuart, 3rd Earl of Bute, typified the contests of political power and the allure of reform in the age of John Wilkes and his battles over parliamentary authority. However, Paine does not simply quote Churchill—he modifies the quotation, and by so emending the couplet from Churchill's "The Author," casts his second *Crisis* paper as a contest of authorial control over an emerging republican print culture. That such contest and control developed under the shadow of a starkly negative poetics is not merely fascinating but instructive in how Paine himself came to view such print republicanism and his own place in both its center and margins.

Chapter 5 starts by looking at Paine's *The Age of Reason*. His deistic masterwork is rarely considered his masterpiece on poetic craftsmanship, yet claims about the scope of imagination, prophecy, and biblical verse, as well as his own very public declamation of poetry as a youthful, inadequate genre for honest political expression make *The Age of Reason* a vital text in the consideration of Paine and poetry, and the source of this book's title. These public claims about the inutility of poetry are, however, paralleled by the fact that Paine was simultaneously writing lyrical poetry in manuscript to the wives of two friends, Robert Smyth and Joel Barlow. Engaging in lyrical practices not unfamiliar to the eighteenth-century's best lyric poets, Paine demonstrates an intense and imaginative poetic sensibility in these poems, and while "The Death of General Wolfe" and "Liberty Tree" are Paine's best-known poems because of their explicitly political content, "From the Castle in the Air to the Little Corner of the World," "Contentment, or If You Please, Confession," and "What is Love" merit serious consideration as Paine's best.

Chapter 6 moves from Paine's known works to the broad swath of poetry written in response to Paine's role in the French Revolution. An entire volume of poetry referencing *Rights of Man* could be compiled and studied over a lifetime (and should be), but my concern here is the poetry that focuses on Paine himself as both bête noire and savior, who because tried in absentia and exiled from England became nothing less than a poetic shibboleth, a convenient vessel for the mass of cultural anxieties that emerged out of English debates in the 1790s concerning the French Revolution and its perpetually threatened importation. Whether about the emergence of women as a political force with claims to the very rights Paine persuasively proclaims, or about the claims of a radical countersphere to genuine political sovereignty, British poetry of the 1790s, often in popular literary genres like broadsides and songsters and by anonymous or unknown poets, invokes Paine as those anxieties' comorbid symptom and cause.

My final two chapters reorient my study toward America and invert the boundaries of literary context. If previous chapters examine Paine's multiple engagements with literary context, these chapters focus on Paine himself as a vital literary context for two important early American poets. In 1995, *Wired Magazine* called Paine the "moral father of the internet."[4] He is no less the godfather of an American poetic tradition exemplified by Philip Freneau and Joel Barlow. Like his influence on the British poetry of the 1790s, Paine's influence on Freneau is couched in an understanding of Paine's character and a reading of Paine's works. Each is calibrated to Freneau's own shifting belief in the value of poetry to America's post-revolutionary political culture and the role poetry could play in the republic as a democratizing instrument. Likewise, Paine's influence on Barlow emerges in the post-revolutionary period. Friends and confederates in the radical American circles that thrived in France during the revolution and the Terror, Paine and Barlow enjoyed a relationship that, though diminished as time went on, lasted until Paine's death in 1809. Paine's impact on Barlow's *The Vision of Columbus* (1787) is best understood through a text: his *Letter to Abbé Raynal* (1782) and its exploration of the early configurations of international cosmopolitanism. Paine's influence on *The Columbiad* is best understood through a theme—not, as one might expect, religion, but rather system. A term used to devastating effect by Paine to decry war and violence in his later writings, it is a poetic cue Barlow takes up in *The Columbiad* in its own prefatorial claims to obviate war and violence. Considered as theme, system demonstrates lasting impact; considered as genre for a poem whose genre has always been its major critical failing, system ultimately offers a reading of the shared critical destinies of Barlow and Paine.

In her novel *Vindication*, a fictionalized life of Mary Wollstonecraft, Frances Sherwood includes a slovenly, inspirational Paine as part of Wollstonecraft's social circle. At dinner one night, Paine says, "Writing is a revolutionary act. . . . You are positing an alternative world, one that was not there before, perhaps an ideal world, whatever you say. By that fact alone, writing is a revolutionary act."[5] Fighter of two revolutions, citizen of the world, invoked phantasm of a twenty-first-century inaugural address, poet with some claim to originality—to this let us add: revolutionary writer, revolutionary poet.

ONE

Wit Is Naturally a Volunteer

Poetry and Print Culture in the *Pennsylvania Magazine*

At a time when considerable progress had been made in printing this volume, the editor was informed that Mr. Paine had sent some contributions to the Pennsylvania Magazine. On which application was made to Mr. R. Aitken, the publisher of that work, who very obligingly pointed out the pieces written by Mr. P. . . . A few other articles, which (Mr. Aitken says) were merely *handed* by Mr. P for publication, have not, on so doubtful a claim, obtained a place here.

—James Carey, advertisement to *The Works of Thomas Paine*

In 1797, James Carey of Philadelphia published the first complete works of Thomas Paine, a two-volume set composed of familiar works and a series of "miscellaneous pieces" drawn exclusively from the *Pennsylvania Magazine* and procured largely by Carey's conversations with its publisher, Robert Aitken. Published between 1775 and 1776, the magazine offered Paine an entry into the literary marketplace of America, a publisher familiar to Paine's patron Benjamin Franklin, and work at a magazine that soon became the most popular in Philadelphia.[1] As such, Paine's role as the magazine's editor from February to July 1775 situated him at the epicenter of an urban literary culture in "the financial and commercial center of the colonies," which witnessed "new classes, particularly the city's artisans, [who] would emerge into political consciousness . . . and often find their voice in Paine's writings."[2] They no less found it in Paine's editing, practiced as an avatar of both literary genre and taste who leveraged poetry in ways radically different from an inherited British magazine tradition that always included poetry amongst its contents. Publishing both his own and others'

7

poetry, often in strategic relations to one another, Paine editorially sought to shape his readers' literary and political "consciousness" while embracing a transatlantic sensibility of an emerging American identity familiar with, and still attached to, British poetry. Paine selected poetry for its political content and as a genre that could do the work of politics in ways prose could not, as well as a space for the early deployments and formations of his political thinking.

In his advertisement for the magazine printed in the November 21, 1774, edition of the *Pennsylvania Packet,* Aitken promised that the fourth section of every issue would be "devoted to the muses. And as mediocrity is more supportable in anything than in poetry, pains will be taken to procure the best and newest essays in this way, always giving preference to the productions of our own country."[3] The focus on quality, novelty, and native American productions would be a consistent narrative of the *Pennsylvania Magazine,* and the job of such poetic procurement fell to Paine as a "novice" editor when he began work on the February 1775 issue of the magazine.

Such magazine editing consisted of more than mere procurement and acquisition. As even Carey's advertisement suggests, Paine had a direct hand in determining the contents of each volume and the general order in which those contents were printed. This is no less than the creation of what Neil Fraistat has called "contexture," or the intricate and interrelated meanings that accrue to accumulated contents, but also the relationships and connections built both within a monthly issue and across a series of issues.[4] What thus emerges is a network of meanings cohering around the editor's work, which controls the literary infrastructure of such meanings in the editor's ability to pick the contents and their placement. Paine's particular power, then, was his ability, through the manipulation of contexture, to shape the magazine's larger narrative that gave "subtle inflection to its meaning[s]" and its overall arguments in favor of the natural political consequence of privileging the literary amongst the products of their own country, which for Paine inevitably became full American independence from Britain.[5] It has been persuasively argued that the *Pennsylvania Magazine* used naturalized, allegorical prose to discuss politics without directly addressing it, and Paine's editing of the magazine's poetry from February to July 1775 insists upon a qualification of that argument.[6] Whether because of poetry's inclination to the imaginative and not the argumentative, its generic demands for more than mere mediocrity, or its status in the magazine as poetical essays, whose "associat[ion] . . . with an easy, unstudied manner . . . between persons of shared social standing" could be leveraged for his own ends, poetry allowed Paine, through both the topics of the poems themselves and their contextural meanings with other pieces, to make more strenuous and open arguments for American independence then he contemporaneously could, or dared, in prose.[7]

These poetic alternatives to prose arguments were evident since Paine's first authorial contribution to the *Pennsylvania Magazine*, which appeared in the first January issue. They were equally conditioned by Aitken's own sense of what his magazine should be. In his advertisement for the magazine in the *Pennsylvania Packet*, Aitken had foregrounded the native attractiveness of his magazine, offering an alternate title ("American Repository of Useful Knowledge") and declaring that "a proportion of nearly the same number of pages in each Magazine will be set apart for original American productions." Aitken's final title, the *Pennsylvania Magazine, or American Monthly Museum*, directs the reader to a specific view of such "original American" values. While the initial "repository" had suggested something nearly identical to "magazine," the magazine as "museum" meant that the material within was collected, and collected in deliberate ways that had to be read against each other as well as displayed in formations "fashioned as a vehicle for the exercise of new forms of power."[8] Those new forms of power were deeply entrenched in the magazine as a literary form and cultural entity affecting those formations through content and readerships,

Illustration from the title page of the *Pennsylvania Magazine*, 1775. (TPNHA Collection, Ryan Library, Iona College)

both of which reflected the eighteenth-century museum movement's embrace of a Habermasian "representative publicness" that allowed the museum to "detach high cultural forms and practices from their functions of courtly display and connected them to new social and political purposes."[9] For Paine, these new "social and political purposes" were bound inextricably to American political independence, and even the vignette heralded on the magazine's title page, "show[ing] the goddess of Liberty holding a shield with the Pennsylvania arms emblazoned on it, [with] a mortar labeled 'The Congress,' battle-axes and pikes, and the word of 'Liberty' on a gorget hanging from a tree, surround[ing] the goddess," reinforces this reading of the magazine as a museum raised to address contemporary social and political realities and invested in the notion of liberty as both a function and product of these museum-generated social and political novelties.[10]

The contrast with other magazines in the colonial era is striking. While those magazines had titles that reflected their chronological frequency or literary genre, the museum was a potent sign of the arguments Aitken wanted to make in terms of America's relationship to her colonial master and how his magazine could shape that relationship. Although Liberty had remained elusive from those items in the vignette, the illustration on the half title page suggests that the contents which follow, especially the poetry symbolized by the lyre, would prop Liberty up and shine, like the light emitted from the assembled objects in the illustration, as a beacon to all its readers. Aitken says as much in his publisher's preface to the magazine's first issue. He proceeds to list the "disadvantages we labour under," which include the infant state of his magazine; the inability of America, as an infant state itself, to provide "discover[y] of the curious remains of antiquity"; and, last, "the principle difficulty in our way, . . . the present unfortunate situation of public affairs." In the absence of such antiquarian products, a central feature of museums fills the gap: a "space of representation" where the creation of cultural meaning rests in the relationship between the objects rather than the antiquity of the objects themselves. This would become centrally important when figured in the *Pennsylvania Magazine* as American ingenuity.[11] Aitken continues, "Those, whose leisure and abilities might lead them to a successful application to the Muses, now turn their attention to the rude preparations for war—Every heart and hand seem to be engaged in the interesting struggle for *American Liberty*. . . . The arts and sciences are not cultivated to advantage, but in the fruitful soil of *Peace*, and in the fostering sunshine of *Constitutional Liberty*." Aitken's attempt at channeling the muses in these final lines invokes the same muses who were linked to

Illustration from the half title to the *Pennsylvania Magazine*, January 1775. (TPNHA Collection, Ryan Library, Iona College)

poetry alone in his original advertisement, and his preface casts his complaints as the very reason for needing an American museum. That America is too young to have any undiscovered antiquities is not so much a cultural disability as a literary and editorial inconvenience answered by the magazine as a call to make those discoveries through reading the magazine itself. Reading and circulating the magazine becomes an inherently political act because it speaks to a prior investment in the American narrative of the magazine. It is then no coincidence that Aitken says it is the muses who would especially suffer and be disabled by the turn to war. If poetry is the subject of such potential danger, then it is poetry that will contend with and contest most the issues that make the American project so fraught with the danger of failure, but also poetry that can simultaneously confront and disseminate the new valences of social and political power that independence represented.[12]

Poetry's ability to contest those political issues and negotiate Aitken's proposed creation of nothing less than an American culture lies in its ability to be a "dynamic process, an ongoing adjustment to and engagement with social and historical content."[13] More so than the static nature of informative articles, or even a set of allegories where figures stand for ideas, that dynamism shared with the museum the objective to fashion and distribute discursive pockets of new forms of power. Reified by the contextual meaning generated from the magazine's relationship between poem and prose, and poem and poem, poetry uniquely was able to embrace and extend the political claims of the magazine. Poetry's form and content equally allowed it to address the sociopolitical concerns of its American audience and likewise to "respond to the often unpredictable energies" of a democracy.[14] Such energies were clearly embedded in the very debates over democracy and independence in 1775.[15] It is not that independence was unthinkable, simply that it was unlikely, and poetry itself had a capacity, "by the sheer nature of its form, to [be] a declaration of opposition of the prevailing consensus."[16] Aitken's hedge in his preface, where American liberty stands within the sunshine of constitutional liberty, reflects his own uncertainty but is also a minor barometer of such consensus. Yet, by claiming a unique role for poetry in his very first advertisement for the *Pennsylvania Magazine*, Aitken inherited a British tradition of including poetry in magazines but devised a significantly different function for it in his museum-magazine. In the vacuum created by the uncertainty of independence as both a political theory and reality for America in 1775, both Paine and poetry would fill the void where existed the possibility of containing and most importantly channeling those democratic "energies" in the very forum provided for them in the magazine, since like the museum, the magazine as museum could inaugurate "power-knowledge relations" that "were democratic in their structure to the degree that they constituted the public they addressed."[17]

Paine picks up this delicate interplay in his first published piece for the magazine. Traditionally called "The Magazine in America," the piece is entitled "The Utility of the Work Evinced." A grab bag of typical prefatorial magazine vocabulary, with references to the magazine's capacity to "entertain" and "improve" and critiques of the diminishing quality of British magazines, Paine's essay achieves such evincing by eloquently arguing for the magazine as an essential instrument and artifact of a young nation, since "a magazine can never want matter in America, if the inhabitants will just do justice to their own abilities." Those abilities, however, operate in a crucial political uncertainty quickly separating itself out from the very concerns Aitken had raised, since "whatever may be our political state, OUR HAPPINESS WILL ALWAYS DEPEND ON OURSELVES." Such affective certainty highlights in relief the lack of political independence that is another source of happiness, and the deflection from current "political states" is followed by his curious description of the American sciences:

We owe many of our noblest discoveries more to accident than wisdom. . . . Such happy accidents give additional encouragement to the making experiments; and the convenience which a magazine affords of collecting and conveying them to the public, enhances their utility. Where this opportunity is wanting, many little inventions, the forerunners of improvement, are suffered to expire on the spot that produced them; and as an elegant writer beautifully expresses on another occasion,

"They waste their sweetness on the desart air"—*Gray*.[18]

It is significant that in his view of the American sciences as "accidental" and in desperate need of an environment in which their experiments could be "collected" and "conveyed," Paine adapts as the summation of America's scientific moment a quote from a poem that includes the line, "Some mute inglorious Milton here may rest" (59). Like Gray's lament of the untapped and unrealized potential made evident by anonymous tombstones in a poor country church, so the American sciences are in danger of being forgotten since they "expire on the spot that produced them." Paine's application of a poetic logic to the failure of the American sciences, but also the potential of the magazine to counter that failure and thus to make scientific progress deliberate, not accidental, points toward the definitional centrality of poetry in the magazine. While scientific discoveries would be collected, and the magazine would create meanings, it is poetry, Paine suggests, even elegy, that makes meaning of those discoveries, and of the magazine's containment of their intertextual collected potential meanings.

The quotation is also transitional, gesturing toward the subsequent paragraphs that will treat Paine's views on the role poetry will play in the magazine's utility, which can be summed up by Paine in a single term: wit. Although on the surface Paine's comments on wit seem to focus on humor, there lies beneath his claims a deeper understanding of the work of poetry in the magazine. He proceeds, "Wit is naturally a volunteer, delights in action, and under proper discipline is capable of great execution. . . . 'Tis a qualification which, like the passions, has a natural wildness that requires governing. Left to itself it soon overflows its banks, mixes with common filth, and brings disrepute upon the fountain. We have many valuable springs of it in America, which at present run in purer streams."[19] As Brean Hammond has written, wit is "a form of capital situated somewhere between the stock of goods or investment funding required to launch oneself in any trading concern and the sump of knowledge improved by mental training required to prepare oneself for a profession," which later "developed into a conception of 'original genius.'"[20] Paine's conception of wit lies somewhere between those two formulations, in part "because [Paine's] theme here is the 'inexhaustible' nature of the arts and sciences, [and] the two sides look closer than they really are."[21] Although not imbued with that romantic notion of originary creative power, Paine's offering of wit, of which "there can be no reason to apprehend a deficiency," is a kind of antidote to the possibility of scientific failure, a "sump of knowledge" not so much for professional preparation as much for poetic salvation. It is wit's fungibility that makes it an essential form of capital, but not one that is authorial in nature so much as poetically formal—that is, accrued to the forms of poetry itself in the magazine. These forms are its very "democratic energies," and precisely why wit is figured as a "volunteer." Rather than experimentation's serendipitous discovery liable to be lost and "deserted," poetry is an agent, a social act, and culturally valuable because it too can be governed. Such governability is precisely the function of poetry in the magazine for Paine, since as part of the museum-magazine's proposed responsibility to shape sociopolitical matters, it offers a reading of culture, much like Paine's own, where "culture might be reorganized in accordance with a governmental logic."[22]

That January volume contains little else of poetic value, and in the subsequent February issue Paine's first poem appears. Entitled "The Snowdrop and the Critic," the poem responds to a suggestion made in the January issue by Aitken in his notice "To The Public": "Thus encompassed with difficulties, this First Number of The PENNSYLVANIA MAGAZINE entreats a favorable reception; of which we shall only say, like the early *snow-drop*, it comes forth in a barren season, and contents itself with modestly foretelling that CHOICER FLOWERS are preparing to appear." In "The Snowdrop and the Critic," Paine personifies the snow drop that portends greater things and pairs it with the critic, whose own place in the cultural and literary landscape was continuously redefined in Paine's era.[23]

Paine has the critic begin,

Prologues to magazines! the man is mad
No magazine a prologue ever had.
But let us hear what new and mighty things
Your wonder-working magic fancy brings. (1–4)

The critic here views the claims of the magazine as mere "wonder-working magic fancy," a critique not so much of the odd generic hybridity of putting prologues, which properly belong to plays, in magazines, but of the magazine itself, whose self-possessed claims of utility are "wonder-working" and thus in this poem "an extraordinary natural occurrence." They are also magical, and thus meant to "manipulate the natural world."[24] "Fancy" here could mean not only the very imagination Paine invokes but also "something imagined," and therefore unnatural and "delusional." The link to "mad" from the first line indicates that the critic's argument reflects an anxiety of failure related to the very stated purposes of the *Pennsylvania Magazine*.

The snow drop thus responds,

> Bit by the muse in an unlucky hour,
> I've left myself at home, and turn'd a flow'r;
> And thus disguis'd come forth to tell my tale,
> A plain white snow-drop gathered from the vale,
> I come to sing that summer is at hand,
> The summer time of wit, you'll understand. (5–10)

Volunteering to stand against "fancy," the snow-drop portends the "summer time of wit" that militates against claims that the magazine is delusional; it is, rather, palpable and therefore governable, with a reference to the potted flower that stands atop each issue's contents page. The poem proceeds to describe how the "garden of our magazine" would "soon exhibit such a pleasing scene,/That even critics shall admire the show" (11–13), and culminates in the exponential growth of the garden such that

> Our numbers, Sir, so vast and endless are,
> That when in full complexion we appear,
> Each eye, each hand, shall pluck what suits its taste,
> And every palate shall enjoy a feast. (19–22)

While the magazine's political allegories "naturalized politics," Paine's poem naturalizes the reception of the magazine itself as a sensory feast, easily digestible by all, no matter their (literal and literary) tastes.[25] The argument is one of sheer volume and magnitude; the magazine cannot be fanciful because it is so plentiful. And that natural plenty is perfectly complemented by the spatial and cognitive precision of its reception and consumption: "each" eye and hand, "every" palate suggests a totalizing reality which rejects the critic's argument that the magazine could ever be merely magical.

This meta-sensory moment generates the most striking feature of the poem: its quasi-dialogic call and response structure of both imagined and real voices, which, coming after the comestible definitions of the magazine, reflect an embedded belief that "the act of criticism suggest[s] not written but oral communication," as well as that "theatricality [is] the essence of natural behavior."[26] Indeed, immediately after the feast enjoyed by every palate, the snow-drop states, "The rose and lily shall address the fair,/And whisper sweetly out—*My dears take care*" (24–25). After this,

> With sterling worth the *plant of sense* shall rise
> And teach the curious to philosophize;
> The keen-ey'd wit shall claim the scented briar,
> And sober cits the solid grain admire;
> While gen'rous juices sparkling from the vine
> Shall warm the audience, till they cry—*Divine:*
> And when the scenes of one gay month are o'er,
> Shall clap their hands and shout—*Encore, encore.* (26–33)

The imagined audience here, performing theatrical responses to horticultural lavishness, are cast as the idealized magazine audience, generating responses governed by the magazine's monthly schedule and lush, natural content. When the critic asks what happens when the frost arrives to kill the vegetation, the snow-drop simply states,

> We'll garnish out the scenes
> With stately rows of hardy ever greens,
>
> . . . .
>
> We'll draw, and paint, and carve, with so much skill,
> That wond'ring wits shall cry—*Diviner still.* (36–37, 40–41)

Like the garden itself, the conditioned responses of the audience, now both "wond'ring" and witty, are gradually improving, but the critic saves his most devastating question for last as a kind of defense against such ameliorating incrementalism:

> But now, suppose
> Some critic wight in mighty verse or prose,
> Should draw his grey goose weapon, dipt in gall.
> And mow ye down, plants, flow'rs, trees, and all. (42–45)

The critic's contention about "mighty" verse and prose is an indication of his already defeated argument: he is already seeing his role in the terms of the snow-drop's definitions of the magazine-as-garden's purpose and role. No less than the audience, the critic's responses, and thus behaviors, have been governed by the magazine's natural delights. The meta-sensory specificity of "each" and "every" inevitably includes the critic who must read to criticize, and the snow-drop's answer is the end-around to the critic's question: "Why then we'll die like flowers of sweet perfume,/And yield a fragrance even in the tomb" (46–47). The movement here is from the generative to the perennial, and, imbued with a kind of staying power that transcends the magazine as literary form and genre, Paine inverts the problem with invention as the solution to any critical attacks on the magazine itself. If scientific invention had suffered from the elegiac tragedy of threatened anonymity in "flowers that in desarts bloom and die," then it is the working of wit, in the poem itself as Paine's first in the magazine, and the suggested natural landscapes of the magazine, that would linger and remain, thus shaping poetry's ability to govern the responses of its readers and critics.

Paine's initial poetic gambit offers poetry as the key to reading the magazine and modulating reader responses. That was a preponderant concern early on for Paine and Aitken, but in the next month's volume, Paine shifts his poetic concerns to what seemed absent from "The Snowdrop and the Critic," namely, an openly political argument concerning the surrounding issues of American liberty and national identity. The result is "The Death of General Wolfe," published for the first time in the March 1775 issue of the *Pennsylvania Magazine,* and the first Paine-written poem that really works the politically contextural abilities of Paine as editor to shape the political message of the magazine. "The Death of General Wolfe" was for Paine a kind of early experiment on the disappearance of Britain as a viable power, and a rejection of elevating Wolfe as a national hero.

The poem's placement amplifies these claims because the March 1775 issue focuses especially on one man: Lord Robert Clive, commander-in-chief of British India. Couched as a kind of mystic vision, the Paine-authored "Reflections on the Life and Death of Lord Clive" portrays him as the scourge of India, since "fear and terror march like pioneers before his camp, murder and rapine accompany it, famine and wretchedness follow in the rear."[27] "Reflections" uses a striking visual and kinetic framework for its description of Clive, as the narrator continually uses "I see" to preface his descriptions, thus invoking the idea that "the visual is associated in the human mind with reality."[28] These reflections aim to reveal the very horrific reality about Clive and his actions. The narrator obligingly follows Clive from England to India and back again repeatedly, with each location crowning Clive. In India, they cower before him, a "spoiler." In England they applaud him, conqueror of the East, but as the narrator reminds the reader, "'tis the peculiar temper of the English to applaud before they think."[29] The narration then shifts to the elderly Clive, a man of deep regret whose physical and mental pains are crippling: "Let us take a view of him in his latter years: Hah! What gloomy Being wanders yonder? How visibly is the melancholy heart delineated on his countenance. He mourns no common care—His very steps are timed to sorrow—He trembles with a kind of mental palsy."[30] An old man broken by his conquering, Clive is regretful of his duty and attachment to England, and haunted by his endless, frenetic movements of return to India to such a degree that he pleads, "Could I unlearn what I've already learned—unact what I've already acted."[31] Clive thus stands, in this same March issue that sees the publication of "The Death of General Wolfe," as a kind of anti-Wolfe. Wolfe's staying power is amplified, specifically because Paine's attempts at celebrating Wolfe are predicated on his refusal to do exactly what Clive does: move. And so, just as Wolfe's Canadian victory is a rejection of Britain, Clive's rejection of Britain, spurred and represented by his constant movement between England and India, is an indictment of the same colonial policies and actions for which Wolfe died.

That March volume thus stands as a real watershed for Paine and poetry in the magazine, a concerted effort to leverage the contextural meanings of the magazine to argue for an increasing distance from England: outright yet unnamed independence. The subsequent April issue contains two interrelated poems used to elaborate and develop what was begun in the March issue. The first is "An Account of the Burning of Bachelor's Hall," identified by Carey as a Paine poem, and "Oh, What a Pity!," which A. Owen Aldridge convincingly argues was written by Paine.[32]

"An Account of the Burning of Bachelor's Hall" constitutes the second of the Old Bachelor series, which Ed Larkin has identified as part of the larger trend in the Bachelor articles, written at times by Paine and occasionally by Francis Hopkinson, "as an analogical context within which such broad ideological problems as consent and independence could be addressed without direct reference to the political relations between the colonies and Britain."[33] Marriage is thus an ideological cipher in the magazine. The first Old Bachelor article appears immediately after "Reflections" in the March issue, and the "Account" picks up where that ends, with the Old Bachelor inviting the reader to visit him again in the bachelor's hall. "An Account," which is unique among the Bachelor series for being the only poem, works to mythologize this second visit:

> Fair Venus so often was miss'd from the skies,
> And Bacchus as frequently absent likewise,
> That the synod began to enquire out the reason,

Suspecting the culprits were plotting of treason.
At length it was found that they had open'd a ball,
At a place by the MORTALS call'd Bachelor's Hall;
Where Venus disclos'd ev'ry fun she could think of,
And Bacchus made nectar for mortals to drink of.
Jove highly displeased at such riotous doings,
Sent TIME to reduce the whole building to ruins.
But time was so slack with his traces and dashes
That Jove in a passion consumed it to ashes. (1–12)

Like Paine's poem "Liberty Tree," "An Account" is clearly modeled on George Alexander Stevens's "Once the Gods of the Greeks." The song evidently held some appeal for Paine as a poetical framework for his early political musings, and by situating the poem within the broader allegorical attempts of the Old Bachelor articles to serve as the magazine's ideological ciphers for sensitive political topics, Paine makes the poem and its mythological ribaldry an inversion of the original song's comments about social politics and liberty. Defined as "treason," the absence of Venus and Bacchus from their Olympian abodes is automatically read as a form of specifically political betrayal, if only because their respective divine attributes, namely love and sex, and wine and revelry, are not identical to the marriage that acts as ideological cipher in this series. Indeed, Venus and Bacchus's merriment is considered "riotous" and thus viewed as necessarily violent and socially destructive by the synodal judgment of the gods. However, it is Jove, as the king of the gods, who acts autonomously and indicts the gods of earthly delights for their near-Promethean error of sharing "nectar" with mere mortals and their "riotous doings." The echo of the "Kings, Commons, and Lords" of "Liberty Tree" resonates deeply with the suspicious synod and autocratic Jove, and Time thus becomes the only deity that can bring the building to ruin and rescind what Venus and Bacchus have taught mortals to "think of" and "drink of." Yet Time is on Venus and Bacchus's side, getting caught up in the delights of the Bachelor's Hall, and Time's "slack" attention, a kind of anti-attraction, to his own "traces and dashes"—both vestige and violence—moves Jove to resort to his own "passions," and the only genuinely violent, destructive act of the poem. While not as incisive as "Liberty Tree," "An Account," through its mythologizing, points to the same broken system of politics that suggests delight as treason and justifies autocratic, monarchical fits of passionate violence. If, then, the discussions of marriage negotiate allegorically the British and American relationship in the other Old Bachelor articles, this poem is its barest prenuptial agreement.

Jove's destructive passion is near allied to the very objects of pity described in Paine's "Oh What A Pity!," a poem exploring the deeper valences of pity as both a necessary and ironic stance toward British colonialism and its American impact:

> When Britain, teeming like an o'er stor'd hive
> Bade her young swarms look about and live,
> The wise advice was relish'd by the brood,
> And each, in distant lands, pursu'd the public good. (1–4)

Paine offers an image of British colonial expansion defined by the relatively benign terms "look" and "live," each of which seek to serve "the public good." The rhyme of "brood" with "good" reflects the kind of intrinsic reading of colonialism Paine engages here, and he continues to chart the global reach of British colonialism as "Some to the rosy east convey'd their all" (5), while "Others, the Indies of the West explor'd" (7) and "Some . . . these milder regions of the north possess'd" (9–10). With the conquest of land comes the subsequent conquest of people, because the British

> Taught nature order, and the heedless flood,
> To land embay'd, where grew perhaps a wood.
> Look here or there, each alter'd spot declares
> It owes its change and fortune to their cares. (15–18)

As the poem progresses, however, the greatest, and most glaring distinctions rest between the fundamentally personal nature of the brood that does good and the ability of their transformative "care" to apply only to the natural world. Paine makes that clear in the next portion of the poem, which takes up the "fair city" (18) where wild animals threaten peace, only for Paine to address "ministers of fate,"

> Who fix the seal to deeds of future date;
> Or ye whose tender office 'tis to mourn
> With friendly sorrows o'er a nation's urn;
> Or ye, whose kindness watching o'er mankind
> Prevent those mischiefs man for man design'd. (28–33)

Paine cedes the natural landscape of the conquered world to the laws and lawgivers who govern it, and to the inevitable misery and destruction that arises from their attempts to control both. Behold empire's downfall, and this downturn of what had started as relatively advantageous British colonial expansion rests on the same terms Paine had instituted at the start of the poem, namely nation and person, such that the British failure to control the latter is precisely what marks its failure in regard to the former.

Paine's poetic framework here is one of diminishing responsibility inversely invested in greater representatives of power and authority. Moving from declining subjects to exuberant bees and from futile ministers of fate to the penultimate stanza's "Ye, one, or all" (34), the poem marks an increasing desperation as it substitutes natural categories (bees and broods) for political (ministers, official mourners) and then general ones (ye, one, or all). It then becomes the responsibility of "ye, one, or all" to "Teach British hearts the power of nature's law,/And kings to know a murder from a war" (36–37). "Nature's law" expresses a belief in an objective set of standards to which the British must not only be held, but must be made to feel an affective acknowledgment. This is a modification of affective consent, not simply "a version of the operations of sympathy, the faculty that puts individuals beyond themselves and their own self-interest into the realm of a mutuality of feelings," but the call to actively inculcate and activate that affective consent through an appeal to "nature's law."[34] Such consensual fashioning also compresses the two subjects of their colonial control (nature and law), which the very call to teach suggests have failed completely. To teach the heart is to appeal to an embedded affective power, to posit the heart as the affective middle between nature and law.[35]

The subsequent lines catalogue, in a sequence of stentorian "shalls," the very reckoning of British colonialism:

Shall these fair plains just rescu'd from woods,

. . . .

become so soon abandon'd and accurs'd?
Shall these fair piles, the work and pride of those

. . . .

Who, when they laid the first foundation stone
Cried, "Bless these labours when we're dead and gone"
Shall these to ruin fall, consume and burn,
And hide with ashes their erectors urn?
Shall groan with groan in dismal concert flow
And Rachael's doleful voice add woe to woe?

Shall street with street unite in gorey streams
And house with house communicate in flames? (38–51)

Never in his poetry does Paine sound so like Oliver Goldsmith, casting British migration as a hazard to the very foundations not just of the nation but of life itself. The "shalls" have a biblical heft to them, accented later by the unique, and somewhat dissonant for Paine, reference to Rachael's cry for her children, although that image's resonance with maternal concern for sons, and sons destined to lead a nation, are appropriate for the poem. If the poem's early lines had focused on the law of diminishing returns and the movement from nature to politics to the heart, then this charts a movement from nature to the heart, from the outside and external to the internal and affective. The internal echo of the *o* emphasis in both "groan" and "woe" both mimics and amplifies the feeling of loss, and from Rachael's laments over her sons Paine moves to the shrinking circle of urban destruction. The transition is admittedly a rough one, but makes sense as the lines absorb the poem's previous imagery of British colonialism as benign nature and spit them out as the destructive urban claustrophobia and human trauma of "gorey streams" and the image of flames that are "communicated" from house to house. "Communicate" circumscribes within its meaning the woeful cries of lines previous but ironically twists the adjunctive features of communication as that which help build community. "Communicate" and "consume" are identical modes and verbs here, each a forceful counter movement that marks the desolate destruction of the American people and the aftermath of British colonial expansion, which untethers every feature of the human landscape from its essential meaning to America.

There is, however, a final "shall":

Shall genuine love in British hearts expire
And nature cease to act 'tween son and sire?
While hell, exulting in the mischief, cries,
There drops a Briton, there a Buckskin dies. (52–55)

No longer does the king's need to distinguish between murder and war have any moral imperative. Again the British heart is invoked, but the poem's greatest pity seems to be that this heart holds no capacity for either nature's law or genuine love. Rachael's maternal concern for her sons has been replaced by the loss of any natural sentiment between "son and sire," and the break of natural affection marks the poem's final assessment and definition of nature. Here it is evacuated of any essential meaning to the relationship between father and son, and by extension, colony and colonial homeland. As Elizabeth Barnes has noted of *Common Sense,* "Paine's revolutionary pamphlet demonstrates the ways in which sympathy may be used to undo previously accepted obligations even as it creates or reinforces others."[36] This poem is the pretext and anticipation of *Common Sense;* this loss of genuine love and all filial connection not only "undoes" the obligation of Americans to a British monarch, it likewise establishes the necessary political precondition for independence, namely separation. Pity, then, is not simply emotional feeling at the loss of such connection; it is the immediate political impetus to the natural consequence and necessary result of British colonial action in America.

Paine's final lines re-invoke Goldsmith to assert various other manifestations of this political impetus:

> Forbid it heav'n, nor let the hasty hand
> Of barb'rous pow'r depopulate the land;
> Let hoary swains in ages yet unborn
> Beneath some village shade, or lonely thorn,
> To list'ning sons the horrid tale proclaim,
> And brand a BRITON with a NERO's name.
> Yet if the parent with a brutal.joy,
> Proceed in arms to murder and destroy,
> May all that's noble call our armies hence
> To stand like men, or fall in brave defence,
> While I disown the place that gave me birth,
> And call my native home *A hell on earth.* (56–67)

These recapitulate the poem's major themes, but encase them in the somewhat displaced Goldmsithian fear of American depopulation, here at the hands of the rapacious British army. Nothing could be so far removed from the poem's opening lines and its focus on the "public good." The "branding" of "a BRITON with a NERO's name" is not as important as the fact that the tale is heard by "list'ning sons," who here have replaced the woeful cries of Rachael with a narrative that, in the absence of a formative relationship between sire and son, becomes the means to "construct the social body" in new (specifically American) ways.[37] These sons have also, crucially, survived the loss of nature between themselves and their "sires," and have poetically replaced both the narrative of loss and British militarism with the need to defend their homeland, the very "streets" and "houses" that were burned. Paine "shows . . . the political expediency of setting limits on the sympathetic imagination," but the limits here are set not by the action of genuine love but the impetus to genuine communication.[38]

The return of "a parent's brutal joy" is the poised affective counterpoint to sympathy, a fit replacement for the vacuum created by both the lack of genuine love and the natural gap between sire and son. The distinction between murder and war urged for the king is again vanished, yet the replacement of parent for the king is no transparent substitution of a named figure for a general one. It is the prelude to the attention Paine pays to both America and England in these final lines, a reckoning for the poem's logic throughout. The subjunctive "may" invests the continental army, the "Buckskins" mentioned earlier, with a nobility represented by the simple binary of standing and falling—with the first representing the abandonment of their status as sons for their character as men, and the second presenting the default condition of America to its colonial master and her soldiers to British colonialism: defense. However, the intrusion of Paine's narrator, the poetic "I," shifts the terms of those conditions to a singular act of conscience, specifically "disowning." The more tangible shift, though, is from America and its multiple responses to British imperialism to the land of Britain itself. While Buckskin sons defend the American homeland, it is Britain the poetic narrator forsakes in terms that highlight the truly piteous in the poem. Because he disowns "the place of [his] birth" and his "native" place, Paine as narrator frames the rejection of England as a "hell on earth" in ironic counterpoise to the hell on earth England is making America. As well, the final lines' utter insistence on the nativeness of Paine to England stresses the point that the lack of relationship between son and sire is not entirely a bad thing; indeed, it shows that "sympathy . . . [is] the basis for democracy, and therefore . . . fundamental to the creation of a distinctly 'American' character."[39] It is, in fact, the one truly genuine opportunity in the poem, for it is the opportunity to disclaim England as surely as it claims America and its citizens. O what a pity, indeed, that something which should be abhorrent, even to nature itself, is that which justifies and instigates the obligatory declamation upon which America's political future and destiny rests.

"O, What a Pity!" marks the *Pennsylvania Magazine* at its most overtly political during Paine's tenure as editor, making claims that insistently impinge on the political debates raging in the colonies. "O, What a Pity!" would be Paine's last poem in the magazine until July 1775, but in the interim the magazine's poetical sentiments on the possibility of American independence did not abate as Paine chose specific poems to highlight the natural consequence of disclaiming his native land and calling it "hell on earth." The June issue includes "Elegy to the Memory of the American Volunteers," a poem signed only "Sylvia" that mourns the American lives lost at the Battle of Bunker Hill in April of that year. It was an event Paine consistently pointed to as the turning point of his own views on independence.[40] The poem recalls and reasserts the idea of "wit" as volunteer. If that poetic virtue had been defined by its governability, and what I have suggested is a modification of affective consent, then here wit has been fully realized by the noble acts of the American volunteers. The poem breezes through its early descriptions of their sacrifice and British guilt, since "The British cheek shall glow with conscious shame" (18), but the American volunteers will be

> dear to every free-born mind,
> Shall need no monument your fame to raise,
> Forever in our grateful hearts enshrin'd;
> And blest by your united country's praise. (25–28)

This living memorial to the fallen volunteers is the affective response to their sacrifice, a calculated riposte to the "conscious" shame and legacy of the British.

Inherent in this sense of shame is the fact that "shame becomes not only a mode of recognition of injustices committed against others, but also a form of nation building."[41] The living monuments to the American soldiers at Bunker Hill stand as the affective pillars of that nation, a response and opposition to the national British body that, in its glowing cheek, reveals that "when shamed, one's body seems to burn up with the negation that is perceived (self-negation); and shame impresses upon the skin, as an intense feeling of the subject 'being against itself.'"[42] The narrator doubts, however, that such embodied shame is genuine affect:

> Our future fate is wrapt in darkest gloom,
> And threatening clouds, from which their souls are free'd,
> E'er the big tempest burst they press the tomb
> Not doom'd to see their much-lov'd country bleed. (45–48)

Indeed, this dark cloud only partially breaks when the narrator reveals that although America is "crown[ed] . . . with Liberty and Peace" (58), it is in a vague, near fatalistic resignation in which true resolution rests:

> To Thee, *Eternal Parent,* we resign
> Our bleeding cause and on thy wisdom rest,

With grateful hearts we bless thy power divine,
And own resign'd *"Whatever is, is best."* (69–72)

As with the reference to Rachael, this religious sentiment and utter reliance on God's providence jars any expectation of Paine's views on religion. And yet for as much as it is excessively providential, if not pious in its sentiments, the poem shares some features with "O, What a Pity!" inasmuch as it tends to invert preexisting relationships. The invocation of the "Eternal Parent" transposes the centrality of the son/sire relationship in that poem, and the substitution of "grateful hearts" for the genuine hearts of "O, What A Pity!" offers a parallel view of the identical issues the poems raise. There is too the matter of the blessing and how that subtly shifts agency in the poem. For the narrator to "bless [God's] power divine" is to invest some intellectual power in the view that "whatever is, is best," but it is also to foreground, and therefore prioritize, the act of blessing as the single most important thing any American could do. This is surely an overtly religious response to the Battle of Bunker Hill, and by all accounts not what Paine himself would believe, but he was, it is clear, perspicacious enough as editor to see that its parallel and complementary narrative about America's political future had a place in his magazine, close to his own "O, What a Pity!"

The June issue also contains an excerpt from a poem by another, better-known poet celebrating the bravery of volunteers in a political cause of freedom: Anna Letitia Barbauld's "Corsica." Barbauld herself would later be an intimate in Paine's social and revolutionary circle in the 1790s, and her own sympathies to political causes allied to Paine's, including American independence, would distinguish her poetic voice from many others.[43] As Paine writes in introducing the poem, "We present our readers with an extract from that justly admired poem, believing it to be applicable to the brave Americans as to our fellow strugglers for liberty, the justly admirable Corsicans." Paine cites lines 132–71 of the 201-line poem, which celebrates the Corsican fight for liberty from British rule, a popular subject of English opposition politics in the 1760s and therefore a source of "valuable insight into opposition politics on the eve of the American War."[44] It is easy to see why Paine chose those lines, since in them "patient hope"

Must wait the appointed hour; secure of this,
That never with the indolent, and the weak
Will freedom deign to dwell; she must be seiz'd
By that bold arm that wrestles for the blessing:

'Tis heaven's best gift and must be bought with blood. (135–41)

This is clearly a more Paine-sympathetic view of "blessing," and given the issue's focus on the Battle of Bunker Hill, the fact that freedom will be "bought by blood" becomes a sadly precise prophecy on the cost of independence for Americans.

As Barbauld continues, the cost of that blood is simple: "heroic deeds,/ And god-like action" (153–54). Barbould tells the reader,

> 'Tis not meats and drinks,
> And balmy airs, and vernal suns and showers
> That feed and ripen minds; 'tis toil and danger;
> And wrestling with the stubborn gripe of fate;
> And war, and sharp distress, and paths obscure
> And dubious. (154–59)

There is a striking nobility in suffering here, and a fashioned desire to follow those paths not so much because they sharpen the mind but because they are performative vessels for "heroic deeds" and "god-like action." As such, the poem becomes a kind of antidote to the suggestions made in "Elegy to the Memory of the American Volunteers," much as the final lines quoted by Paine militate against the notion that whatever is, is best:

> And when [Freedom's] sons in that rough school have learn'd
> To smile at danger, then the hand that rais'd
> Shall shush the storm, and lead the shining train
> Of peaceful years in bright procession on. (167–70)

The lovely cascade of *sh* sounds in "shall" and "shush" contrasts with the "storm" that in the poem represents the deleterious fog of war. That tonal clash becomes beautifully resolved by the "shining train" which strings those same sounds together in an aural harmony that perfectly embodies the image it describes. Likewise, the inverted diction of the last line and Barbauld's encasing of it in two prepositions betrays the uncertainty in her own bold claims. It appears, then, that Paine chose these lines specifically for their inherent hope but also for the doubt and trepidation embedded within them.

In an issue of the *Pennsylvania Magazine* that also includes an elegy whose doubts are more secure because more religious, but far less inspirational, the poem itself is truly "just," as Paine emphasizes in the introduction.

It pays justice to the American volunteers who died at Bunker Hill, imbuing their deaths with deeper meaning to the cause of freedom and independence, but also pays justice to the less than perfect state of independence's cause by mid-1775. That too is why equally if not more important than Barbauld's poem is the fact that she, styled as "Miss Aitkin," her maiden name, is the poet excerpted. Immediately before the lines quoted, Paine reprints the 1773 *Monthly Review* assessment of the poem and the volume in which it was first published. It celebrates her "justness of thought," which Paine plays with in his introduction by repeating the word "justly" to describe the poem's sentiments, yet it also reveals something very peculiar about Barbauld's poetry. Paine writes, "The extraordinary merit of this poetic enchantress has made even the monthly reviewers polite."[45] He then quotes from the *Monthly Review:* "When this fair Form offered herself, attended by a train of virtues, so pleasing, so enchanting, . . . we lost the rage of our peculiar devotion, and, from cruel and snarling critics (as all *Reviewers* are known to be) were metamorphosed into happy and good-tempered men."[46] The power of Barbauld's poetic enchantment is her affective turn, her ability to shape the inner characters and private emotional concourses of the reviewers. And while this, and the very public call for freedom and freedom-fighting Barbauld issues in "Corsica," situates her firmly in the middle of a critical discourse that pulls her in differing directions, for the purposes of Paine in the *Pennsylvania Magazine,* such an interpretation of Barbauld's poetry, and Barbauld as poet, fits squarely into the work of poetry that has been traced from "The Snowdrop and the Critic" through to "O, What a Pity!" and "Elegy to the Memory of the American Volunteers." It is precisely her affectiveness that Paine seeks to recruit as much as her very public sympathies to Paine's own cause of independence and eventually revolution. It is precisely her abilities to reform male manners upon which Paine is keen to draw, not as anything other than that which will make them sympathetic to and intellectually attuned to his and the magazine's calls for independence from Britain, if not as stated fact then as necessary and justified consequence of their many poetic arguments. It is her role as both advocate and ally of the magazine's and Paine's political causes that "justly" places "Miss Aitkin" in the context of Paine's penultimate issue as editor.

The July 1775 issue of the *Pennsylvania Magazine* would be Paine's last as editor.[47] It ended, fittingly, with Paine's "Liberty Tree," "the best lyrical expression of this man of prose," rooted in an issue published one year before the Declaration of Independence.[48] In what would be his final manipulation of contexture, Paine links his poem not simply to "The Account of the Burning of Bachelor's Hall," with which it shares a common source, but also to a series of short articles that had appeared intermittently in Paine's tenure as editor but with increasing frequency in his final issues overseeing the magazine. The first of these articles, entitled "Instances of English Longevity," appears in the February 1775 issue and relates the story of Thomas Par, who "died in London in the year 1635, aged 152 years." It also tells the story of Henry Jenkins, who "died in Yorkshire in 1670, being at that time seventeen years older than his contemporary, Thomas Par, viz. 169."[49] The article is anecdotal myth making, and includes an important note at the end: "As there is a secret pleasure in preserving these venerable instances of longevity, The Publisher will be obliged to any of his Correspondents, who will favour him with well authenticated accounts of a similar kind; and the more so if AMERICAN ones."

The correspondents came through. The next article would not appear until the May 1775 issue, entitled "A Remarkable Instance of AMERICAN LONGEVITY" and relating the story of a Maryland man whose age "was by accident lost" but who was certainly "a man and in London at the public entry of King William and Queen Mary, in 1688."[50] The casually dropped point of reference is certainly not accidental; the ascension of William, marking the end of the Glorious Revolution, marks a watershed moment for the revolutionary model that was imminent in America itself. Pragmatically, the article is another claim of America's independence from, and in this case equality to, England as a land of such longevity, even if its reference point is still a particularly English moment of history. The next article, "A Remarkable Instance of American Increase," appearing in the June issue, shifts the ground of exceptionalism slightly, as it suggests that the titular instance "perhaps hath never been exceeded in any age or country in the world." The uniqueness of the incident as much as its increase held up as vital, the article continues, "A poor widow woman of this province, being left with child by her husband, lay in with twins. Soon after this she married a second time, and in less than a twelve-month from the birth of her twins, she brought her husband *four* children at one birth."[51] In an issue generally dedicated to commemorating American losses at the Battle of Bunker Hill, and which includes Barbauld's poetic paean to the high cost of freedom and Sylvia's elegiac lament at the bloodshed necessary for an uncertain future, the woman's peculiar gynecological stamina is meant to be a boon and a contrast to those American losses at Bunker Hill, providing new "Buckskins."

The July issue possesses the final article in this series, titled "Remarkable Instance of American Longevity." Coming as it does in the same issue as

Paine's "Liberty Tree," the article is notable not only for its length, being nearly twice as long as any of the others, but also for its subject: "John Ange, a planter, between *Broad-Creek* and the head of *Wicomoco* river in swampy grounds, at that time reputed *Maryland,* now of the territories of *Pennsylvania,* died about five years ago, aged one hundred and forty years . . . Both he, and his father were of lean constitutions and lived poor and sparing; *i.e.* on *simple and natural Food;* not the *nerve-destroying Teas* and *Coffee;* not kept in perpetual fevers by strong *Madeira,* nor provoking a sickly appetite by rich and *high-seasoned Dishes.*"[52] This most unique, exemplary model of American longevity is, of course, a planter, one whose job it is to plant trees like liberty's. As well, the general discouragement from the drinking of tea echoes the February issue's "Substitutes for Tea," which had argued that "if we must, through custom, have some warm tea, once or twice a day, why may we not exchange this slow poison . . . for teas of our own American plants; many of which may be found, pleasant to the taste and very salutary."[53] So "salutary" that one could live until one hundred and forty, apparently, but the article reinforces the medicinal benefits of native soils to the planter at a very specific and contexturally strategic point in the magazine. As Ed Larkin has noted, "It is not the weakening of the body, but the debilitating effect the importation of tea from Britain has on the body politic" that serve as the primary argument of "Substitutes for Tea," and this article offers the inverse: the rejuvenating and invigorating power the native soil has on the American body. It is in nothing less than such native soil that Paine's liberty tree must grow.[54] And as Paine's "Liberty Tree" persuasively argues for new forms of sociability that invested an unnamed nation with the unique democratic power to support and sustain liberty, then the poem's contextural situation in the July issue of the *Pennsylvania Magazine* leaves no room for interpretation. That country is no less than an independent America.

TWO

Speak of It as It Is

Forms of Liberty in Paine's Early Poetry

What, then, it may be asked, is to be done with Mr. Paine's reputation
as a poet. We answer, "speak of it as it is"—treat it as it deserves.

—*Port Folio*, vol. 6, no. 5, 1815

I n what thus far has been the only scholarly treatment of Thomas Paine's
poetry, A. Owen Aldridge in "The Poetry of Thomas Paine" proclaims,
"Even the most fanatical devotees of Thomas Paine have had very little to
say concerning his verse," and the history of various Paine editions from
James Carey's in 1797 through to Philip Foner's in 1945 have proved Aldridge correct.[1] However, in the years immediately after his death, it seems
Paine enjoyed a better reputation for poetry than he would over the next
two centuries. A prime example of this critical response to Paine's poetry
comes from the *Port Folio*, a literary and political magazine founded by Jo-
seph Dennie and Ashbury Dickens. Its 1815 edition included an anonymous
article portentously entitled "Remarks on the Pretensions of Thomas Paine,
Author of 'Common Sense,' to The Character of a Poet." The roots of such
pretension, the author proclaims, lie in the praises Paine apparently received
for his poetry: "The poetical talents of Mr. Paine, have been long, and
in no slight degree, extolled in this country, and we believe in Great Britain
also, on account of his famous song on the death of general Wolfe."[2] Even
accounting for the author's penchant for hyperbole, that Paine was ever held
in such high regard as a poet, or was so for that length of time, is intriguing
as well as curious, but not so is the fact that the focus of poetical criticism
on Paine has centered on his early poem "The Death of General Wolfe."
Published for the first time in the March 1775 volume of the Paine-edited
Pennsylvania Magazine, that poem, as well as his "Liberty Tree," published

first in the July volume, is an ideal subject for examining how he translated his editorial handling of poetry at the magazine into his own poetic craft. Paine reveals an acute sensitivity to his contemporary poetry, a willingness to facilely adapt poetic tropes and figures, and a firm belief in the ability of poetry to explore and transmit inchoate political values and concepts.

As my previous chapter indicated, Paine cultivated his poetical editorship of the *Pennsylvania Magazine* to proffer those inchoate values, and in no poem more so than his own "Liberty Tree." If "The Death of General Wolfe" became synonymous with Paine as poet in the years during and after his death, then "Liberty Tree" is the poem that defined his poetic legacy as his most anthologized poem. The image of the liberty tree is not unique to Paine, and while "the furor created by the passage of the Stamp Act [1765] . . . begot the original Tree of Liberty," it is instead a contemporary song from which Paine drew the inspiration and source material for his own poetic liberty tree.[3] His poem was published in the *Pennsylvania Magazine* with the note "Tune, The Gods of the Greeks," a reference to a song first published in George Alexander Stevens's *Choice Spirit's Chaplet, or, Poesy from Parnassus* in 1771. Stevens was an actor and sometime comedian, "for many years a strolling player," and most famous for his *Lecture on Heads*.[4] His song, listed by its first line in the table of contents, merits printing in full:

The Origins of British Liberty

BY GEORGE ALEXANDER STEVENS

Once the gods of the Greeks, at ambrosial feast,
Large bowls of rich nectar were quaffing;
Merry Momus among them was fat as a guest,
(Homer says the celestials lov'd laughing:)
On each in the synod the humourist droll'd,
So none could his jokes disapprove;
He sung, reparteed, and some smart stories told,
And at last thus began upon Jove.

"Sire! Atlas, who long has the universe bore,
Grows grievously tired of late;
He says that mankind are much worse than before,
So he begs to be eas'd of their weight."
Jove, knowing the earth on poor Atlas was hurl'd,
From his shoulders commanded the ball;

Gave his daughter Attraction the charge of the world,
And she hung it up high in his hall.

Miss, pleased with the present, review'd the globe round,
To see what each climate was worth;
Like a di'mond, the whole with an atmosphere bound,
And she variously planted the earth:
With silver, gold, jewels, she India endow'd;
France and Spain she taught vineyards to rear;
What suited each clime on each clime she bestow'd,
And FREEDOM she found flourish'd here.

Four cardinal virtues she left in this isle,
As guardians to cherish the root;
The blossoms of LIBERTY 'gan for to smile,
And Englishmen fed on the fruit:
Thus fed, and thus bred, from a bounty so rare,
O preserve it as free as 'twas giv'n.
We will while we've breath; nay we'll grasp it in death
Then return it untainted to heav'n.

Predicated on a joke, Stevens's version of British liberty is divine in origin but satiric and censorious in content. It is Momus's own version of equality, here his willingness to mock everyone in the "synod," that occasions the bestowal of liberty. It is furthermore motivated by the Atlean willingness to unburden himself of the globe because "mankind are worse than before." Human degeneracy necessitates liberty, and liberty itself is a corrective to human behavior. It is Jove's daughter Attraction who becomes responsible for the globe, but instead of supporting and shouldering it like Atlas, she "hung it up high in [Jove's] hall." This move from a male supporter to a female guardian and from a world held up to a world displayed allows Attraction to bestow her gifts on each "clime" and to view the world for its inherent value, not its valuation through Atlas's assessment of humanity.

Accordingly, she views the world not as a burden but "like a di'mond," encircled with an atmosphere that in turn contains what she will list as those countries with the greatest forms of capital, although they each have a special relationship to England. England's crown jewel colony gets material wealth, its continental contenders get their oenological richness, and England itself gets the more valuable political capital: "FREEDOM." Stevens, though, is careful to show that while each country's riches and gifts are explicitly gifted and given, "endow'd and taught," freedom in England is "found." Indeed, Attraction "bestows" on each clime only what "suits" it, but freedom is clearly more suited to England than jewels to India or wine to France because it is what England always already had.

Freedom in the last stanza becomes liberty and takes on a decidedly arboreal character, taking "root," blossoming, and feeding Englishmen, with the only admonition being to "preserve it as free as t'was given." That single ethical stricture extends from life to death, when the imperative is not to preserve but to "return" it. There are then two parallel continuums posited in that final stanza as the living context for English liberty, whose origin is also its end. "Preserve" and "return" form the first continuum, the inclinations and acts by which English liberty exists for Stevens. The other, amplified by the rhyme, is the liberty upon which Englishmen are "fed" and "bred." The comestible and the oenological are one; liberty does not merely sustain but generates Englishmen who will inevitably act as its emissaries by embodying the very liberty they have consumed. This, then, is how the goddess Attraction earns her name: necessarily drawing things together, she assures that English liberty's roots, agents, and end are ultimately one.

Paine's clear familiarity with this song helps us to understand the democratic impulses inherent within his own poem. He opens by framing the genealogy of liberty:

> In a chariot of light, from the regions of day,
> The Goddess of Liberty came,
> Ten thousand celestials directed her way
> And hither conducted the dame.
> A fair budding branch from the gardens above,
> Where millions with millions agree,
> She brought in her hand as a pledge of her love,
> And the plant she named Liberty Tree. (1–8)[5]

The "ambrosial feast" has been replaced by strikingly luminescent imagery and Attraction by the Goddess of Liberty. Emerging "from the regions of day" in "a chariot of light" the Goddess of Liberty is herself a gift, and that riot of light is fundamentally democratic: "ten thousand celestials directed her way" from the "gardens above / Where millions with millions agree." These are wonderfully peculiar poetic renderings of what grassroots democracy looks like for Paine, the work of each individual acting in concert in an act of political will. As well, this vision of the celestials stands in contrast to

Stevens's "synod," which, with its religious overtones, implies a hierarchical imposition of liberty upon the British.

That contrasting sensibility is furthered by the Goddess of Liberty's "pledge of . . . love." Such a pledge is the product of a democratic power sharing "society" from which many thousand celestials equally "direct" her, but a pledge is not a gift, and love is not attraction. Love here is the sentimental rationale for the pledge, not something that draws together but that which guarantees the terms of the pledge. The pledge in turn is not the oenological and comestible wonder of Stevens's poem; instead, it has within it a sense of moral responsibility and duty, and of something given as security for something even greater than the pledge itself.[6] It subsequently behooves those to whom the pledge is given to act in specific ways toward the pledger and the pledge, in this case, the Liberty Tree.

This is Paine's poetic rendering of political responsibility, of what the individual owes to both liberty and whatever as yet politically unspecified form the protection of that liberty will take. Liberty is not a corrective, nor is it a complete gift to which the individual bears no political or social responsibility. Instead, the individual, and later society, enters into a relationship with the Goddess by which they are made part of a contract, the terms of which they are morally obligated to fulfill. This is a greater and better burden than the world upon Atlas's shoulders, and Paine continues in the next stanza:

> The celestial exotic stuck deep in the ground,
> Like a native it flourished and bore;
> The fame of its fruit drew the nations around,
> To seek out this peaceable shore.
> Unmindful of names or distinctions they came,
> For freemen like brothers agree;
> With one spirit endued, they one friendship pursued
> And their temple was Liberty Tree. (9–16)

Liberty becomes a secular religion, and the land "where freemen like brothers agree" is the genuine synod, endued with a single spirit and not one imposed by the gods. "Native" arises again, as it will in "The Death of General Wolfe," but here it is used not as adjective but as simile. The liberty tree is stranger; the liberty tree is authentically alien to England, not suited to it. But it nonetheless finds root in England, where it "flourishes" and "bears" like Stevens's liberty but without the nationalistically generative properties.

As well, I would suggest that having established love as the preeminent idea and act of the Goddess of Liberty, Paine is in this stanza showing the real "attraction" of liberty, since it "drew the nations round,/To seek this peaceable shore./Unmindful of names or distinctions they came." If in Stevens's poem Attraction is a figure of distinction, identifying each distinct "clime" and assigning them their gifts through difference, then Paine's attraction, the product of love and the very content of the Goddess's pledge, is a leveler, pulling the whole globe toward the liberty tree and in so doing reducing if not outright eliminating social distinctions that impede liberty and political unity.

This, then, is why "freemen like brothers agree," just like the celestial "millions" who "with millions agree." The second simile in the stanza, it is predicated on the first. Just as the Liberty Tree adapts easily "like a native," so too does liberty, fruit of that tree, eradicate social distinctions to the degree that those who because of it become freemen act like brothers. Freemen are created not out of explicitly political acts or institutions but because of the social leveling of liberty, which any political system must assure, since its very existence and authority will be dependent upon the basic political consensus of such freemen. And this consensus is crucial because it preserves the difference in distinction from the celestials who don't agree "like" anything but simply agree.

This consensus motivates and impels those freemen to act on behalf of liberty—in short, to fulfill their part of the first stanza's "pledge of love." Paine further distances his poem from Stevens's by suggesting that "Their bread in contentment they ate,/Unvexed with the troubles of silver or gold,/The cares of the grand and the great" (18–20); but in echoes of his "Death of General Wolfe," those freemen

> With timber and tar ... Old England supplied,
> And supported her power on the sea:
> Her battles they fought, without getting a groat,
> For the honor of Liberty Tree. (21–24)

The lines may seem surprising given their publication date of 1775, with Paine poetically imagining an ancient English liberty that is protected by the military service and sacrifice of freemen. Yet the description of England as "old" and the invocation of honor push the poem to its conclusion:

> But hear, O ye swains ('tis a tale most profane),
> How all the tyrannical powers,

Kings, Commons, and Lords, are uniting amain
To cut down this guardian of ours.
From East to the West blow the trumpet to arms
Thro' the land let the sound of it flee:
Let the far and the near all unite with a cheer,
In defense of our Liberty Tree. (25–32)

While this poem ostensibly concerns English liberty, it ultimately does not. "Freemen like brothers agree" to defend the land of the liberty tree and the liberty tree itself, not for a "groat" but as the condition they must fulfill for the Goddess of Liberty's pledge of love in the form of the liberty tree. The exercise of that moral and political responsibility is built around consensus, which is an attribute of both the celestials who bring the liberty tree and those who find "contentment" around it. That was the state of things for "old" England. Now, in the final stanza, it is not freemen, but the institutional machinery of ostensibly "new" England that seeks to cut down the liberty tree and eradicate not social difference but liberty itself. Paine's ordering of the "tyrannical powers" reads like an obscene attraction—three levels of institutional authority, including the "commons" who ostensibly speak for and represents the people, colluding conspiratorially to abscond with liberty in all its forms. "Kings, Commons, and Lords" here "unite amain," with "unite" becoming a highly artificial gathering in contrast and contradiction to the mutual and meaningful "agreement" of celestials and freemen with each other.[7] That the institutional representatives of England's political authority unite "amain" is equally crucial for Paine, since the word suggests a coming together both in great haste—which makes this a kind of ad hoc arrangement whose structure and purpose are illegitimate in contrast to the long tradition of English liberty—and in great numbers, with the combined members of the monarchy, commons, and lords contrasted with both the "millions" as well as with the innumerable freemen who come from across the globe to stand by the liberty tree.[8]

This emphatic criticism of Paine's contemporary English political system necessitates another of his deviations from Stevens's poem: the liberty tree's guardianship. In Stevens's original, it is "four cardinal virtues" sent "as guardians to cherish the root," with liberty being the value that needs protecting. The humans who need it as corrective in the gift economy of that poem never really possess it. Here, in what seems to be the condition the Goddess of Liberty accepted with her pledge, it is the tree itself that is guardian; it is a liberty tree put to the service of the freemen whose social status is defined by it, and to which their acts of protection are all devoted. This designation of the liberty tree as a guardian invests the final lines with their energy and impulse. If the word "amain" suggests both strength in raw numbers and a merely occasional quality to the unholy trinity of "Kings, Commons, and Lords," then the geospatial references of the final lines recall both the "seeking" of other nations and Paine's final assessment of Stevens's claim that Attraction grants liberty. As Paine writes in a letter to Thomas Jefferson: "Attraction is to matter, what desire is to the mind; but cohesion is an entirely different thing, produced by an entirely different cause—it is the effect of the figure of matter.... While I consider attraction as a quality of matter capable of acting at a distance from the visible presence of matter, I have as clear Idea of it as I can have of invisible things.... No visible figure can explain attraction."[9] It is not attraction but "cohesion" that draws free-men together in parallel directions, "from East to West" and "far and near." Global distances are collapsed, and even Paine's use of "flee," typically associated with running away, reflects a deeper sense of something that "hastens for safety and protection."[10] This collapse of global distances, the necessary corollary of liberty's earlier, prior collapse of social distinctions, also allows those who fall under its sway to "unite with a cheer." Within the space of four poetic lines, Paine has repeated the word that marked the "Kings, Commons, and Lords" as distinct from those groups touched most intimately by the liberty tree and the Goddess' pledge. What, then, has changed, so that this use of "unite" is different from the first? "Cheer" seems to be one answer, since it condenses the entire framework of Stevens's poem and renders it as the prevailing attitude and mindset of those who defend the liberty tree—character and not context.

The other answer, I would suggest, is a return to an associational world which will offer Paine a vision for his "Death of General Wolfe." In their agreement, both the celestial millions and millions as well as the freemen as brothers had united prior to agreeing. The terms of their agreement were predicated on a prior act or idea: for celestials, the emergence of a literal enlightenment liberty, and for the freemen, a commitment to that liberty, no matter their national origin. For those freemen in particular, such liberty had drawn them, but it had also defined them, investing their commitment to the liberty tree with a conviction that informed their actions. The need to defend the liberty tree comes only after they agree about the nature and extent of liberty and the level of their commitment to it. They "agree" before they "unite," and that unity takes the form of an associational bond that sees them coming together from all corners of the globe to serve a common cause. As Peter Clark writes, "Clubs and societies may have served as a vector for new ideas, new values, new kinds of social alignment, and forms of national, regional, and local identity."[11] What Paine presents in this final stanza of "Liberty Tree" is nothing less than a global club. Limned by East and West and reaching "far and near," this global association surrounds its primary mission to defend the liberty tree with the constellation Clark suggests: new ideas, such as casting the king himself as equally responsible for the loss of England's ancient liberty; new social alignments that in the poem are dependent upon the eradication of class distinctions and a special kind of cohesion; new values such as a concept of liberty that is not a function of war but a sociopolitical reality that must be vigorously defended by those who benefit most from it; and new forms of nationalism, which arise incipiently in this final stanza but are not explicitly named. However, it seems clear that by the end of the poem, England can no longer fulfill the obligations set forth by the Goddess of Liberty since its freemen are radically separated from their representative political institutions. What less is Paine envisioning in this final stanza, then, than a new national formation that could fulfill the obligations that cohere around a "pledge of love"? The poem's publication in the July 1775 edition of the *Pennsylvania Magazine* confirmed what exactly that national formation was: nothing less than the United States of America.

The apparent darling of Paine's extant poetry critics, "The Death of General Wolfe" serves as the poetic counterpoint to "Liberty Tree" because it espouses a parallel set of values and propositions. It likewise situates itself askance from the virtual subgenre of poetry that grew around Wolfe's death, for reasons that have to do with Paine's interest in using poetical genres as political forums, but also because the poem was likely first performed, or at least written by Paine, while he was a member of the Headstrong Club of Lewes in the late 1760s. This unique convergence of factors—namely, a poem written about a celebrated British war hero who became an emblem of British patriotism; a poem whose genre defies singular definition because it occasionally occupies various categories like elegy, fable, and ballad; a poem upon which Paine's poetical character, as far as it goes, is hung; and a poem deeply embedded in a club environment that Peter Clark suggests created an "associational world"—means that "The Death of General Wolfe" merits critical scrutiny as partner to "Liberty Tree" and Paine's assessment of the contested nature of British liberty.

The poem begins "In a mouldering cave where the wretched retreat,/ Britannia sat wasted with care" (1–2). There,

She mourned for her Wolfe, and exclaim'd against fate
And gave herself up to despair.
The walls of her cell she had sculptured around
With the feats of her favorite son;
And even the dust, as it lay on the ground,
Was engraved with the deeds he had done. (3–8)[12]

The *Port Folio* writer damns with faint praise: "This stanza, although certainly the least exceptionable in the song, is by no means faultless."[13] The stanza, however, is more complex than the *Port Folio* writer, or history, has it. Paine capitalizes on the elegy's characteristic emotional extravagance, with Britannia, a familiar figure in other Wolfe poetry, languidly mourning her lost son Wolfe and desperately trying to memorialize him with "sculptured" images that, on her cell walls and in dust, are simultaneously permanent and yet evanescent. Paine seems unsure whether the dust is engraved because Britannia has scrawled more images into it, or because the dust, as cast-off detritus from her sculptured walls, also holds "the deeds he had done" as a kind of powdery echo of the rocky sculpting that occupies her self-induced imprisonment. Yet Britannia seems strangely uncomforted by the sculptures; her making does not comfort her mourning, and the ambivalence of the testamentary act resists any attempts to make this a poem that simply romanticizes Wolfe as an emblem of liberty or British military might. Such ambivalence is embedded in Paine's very choice of dusty memorializing; while a great portion of contemporaneous Wolfe poetry expressed "fear of the disintegration of Wolfe's monument," Paine's imagery emphasizes its disintegratory nature.[14]

Peter Clark has suggested that the growth of clubs and other social environments in the eighteenth century created an "associational world" in which clubs "helped to engender a more integrated British social space encompassing the British Isles and nascent empire."[15] Paine's opening stanza refines that space very carefully, offering both a "mouldering cave" and a "wretched retreat," the latter of which is wretched because it is mouldering from the neglect occasioned by Wolfe's death. The cost of empire and its integration, while noble, is high. Indeed, such space is not in Paine's poem impersonal; there is nothing, as the *Port Folio* writer suggests, "extravagant" in "the representation of Britannia wearing herself down to the condition of a mummy, neglecting all other considerations, and resigning herself to absolute despair, on account of the death of one man."[16] That, in fact, is the very point of Paine's poem. The individual within the integrating, if not yet fully integrated, social space of the poem does indeed have a profound impact upon the state of the nation and its potential for stability.

This is surely a seed of Paine's eventual arguments for the democratic potential of the individual in his later political writing, as well an early instance of what has been called Paine's penchant for the "melodrama of isolation in embryo."[17] In the next stanza, he moves beyond the space of the "wretched retreat" and ascends into the heavens:

The sire of the Gods, from his crystalline throne,
Beheld the disconsolate dame,
And moved with her tears, he sent Mercury down,
And these were the tidings that came:
"Britannia forbear, not a sigh nor a tear
For thy Wolfe so deservedly loved,
Your tears shall be changed into triumphs of joy,
For thy Wolfe is not dead but removed." (9–16)

The invocation of the divine Greek panoply introduces an important element of fable to the poem, which Paine foregrounded in his introduction to the poem when it appeared in the *Pennsylvania Magazine.*[18] Wolfe's selection by the gods for "removal," not death, marks such removal as vastly more important than mere "tidings" of consolation for Britannia and signals that something else is at work. As Annabel Patterson writes: "For the fable to do its work in the world, a contemporary vocabulary and issues cannot merely be grafted upon a traditional matrix, but the past and the present must be seen to be *structurally* related. And the more people wrestled to accommodate received systems to vast social and cultural changes, the more it became evident that the fable was no rudimentary signifying system, but capable of doing advanced work in the arena of political definition."[19] Patterson's structural relation is Clark's "integrated social space" in Paine's poem, but as suggested by the ambivalence of Britannia's memorial, Paine is intent on problematizing those spaces and relations. The intimacy between Britannia and Wolfe engenders a specific kind of bond between the nation and the individual, and Britannia's grief cements the connection between the past she represents and the present, which Wolfe represents in both victory and death. Neither are "structures" per se, and Paine's insistence on the personal cost to Britannia shifts the focus from those structural connections to more natural and less abstract ones.[20] That explains the stanzaic order of the poem and why Britannia's mourning is both interrupted and consoled by the arrival of Mercury. They are together the "traditional matrix" upon which Wolfe's legacy and glory is affixed, but it is the deeply affective relationship between Britannia and Wolfe, past and present, nation and individual, that precedes and authorizes the quasi-salvific intervention of Jove through Mercury.

This is precisely how Paine offers new "political definitions" through the fable elements in the poem. Wolfe's "removal" serves as a deliberate counterpoint to Britannia's engraving; whereas she seeks to paradoxically memorialize him both permanently and temporarily, he achieves immortality in a strange kind of displacement that reads like a secular assumption. That assumption is ultimately a greater legacy than Britannia's wasted testamentary acts and suggests that Wolfe's individual accomplishment is greater than any single, failed act of national memorialization. That attempt at nationalized mourning is vitiated by what Wolfe's individual sacrifice does to secure his relationship to Britannia and thus the relationship of present to past. It is, politically, the individual actor who achieves the synthesis of the elements (past, present, and matrix) necessary to make any significant claim to political definition. Indeed, if in the general discourse of British patriotic poetry, Britannia was represented as "protected by God and Nature from the rest of the world by rocky cliffs," thus establishing England's political uniqueness and Englishmen's status as the chosen ones, then Paine inverts this by having Britannia wretched and mournful while Wolfe alone is protected and prosaically "removed."[21] It is person not *patria* that merits divine approbation, and for Paine Britannia can only receive the same secondarily and vicariously, if at all.

This is why Wolfe's death, though suffered for Britannia, is by the poem's end only narrated to her, turned into a story she is told and not one she authors in any meaningful way. The power to remember and thus celebrate is removed from her and her own ambivalent testaments to Wolfe are replaced by a divine narrative. This too is Paine's attempt at using the fable to make new political definitions, as Wolfe's "removal" is ultimately spurred by the very same activity that claimed him on earth: war, specifically between the gods and titans. Thus,

He begg'd for a moment's delay;
He cry'd "Oh! forbear, let me victory hear,
And then thy command I'll obey."
With a darksome thick film I encompass'd his eyes,
And bore him away in an urn,

Lest the fondness he bore to his own native shore,
Should induce him again to return. (26–32)

Once again, the *Port Folio* critic supplies a useful response: "If any thing had been wanting to complete the climax of absurdity which marks this ballad, it is amply supplied in the four last lines. Where, we will not say in elegiac, but even in mock heroic poetry, can we find a more forced conceit, or a more ludicrous representation, than that of Mercury deliberately blind-folding the ghost of general Wolfe, cramming it into an urn, and, when thus disposed of, carrying it off under his arm, for the purpose of having it ap-pointed generalissimo of the celestial armies?"[22] Once hyperbolic, now sar-castic, the *Port Folio* writer nonetheless offers a keen insight into precisely the kind of "work" Paine is doing with his poetical fable. While the *Port Folio* critic sees Wolfe's removal to lead the celestial armies as "a caricature attempt at the sentimental sublime," the fact that Wolfe is designated for such lofty service is precisely how Paine attempts to shift political categories away from traditional lines of authority and, as the bellicose context of Wolfe's service exemplifies, the roots of all political authority.[23] If in Greek myth the war between gods and titans is the event that consolidates and asserts the gods' power over both the natural and supernatural order, while simultaneously demonstrating the structural relation between the past and the present through their familial metaphors, then Paine has already, in a poem with displacements and removals, generated new structural connec-tions and conditions within Britannia's affective sentiment for he whom she must memorialize but cannot. By making Wolfe, the human actor in the contemporary drama, the exalted chief of the celestial armies, Paine is advocating for precisely what that image suggests: not simply a politics in which the natural human order supersedes any claim to the supernatural origin of political power, but one in which the origin of all political power rests in the individuals' relations and not in any institution or structure prior to those individuals.

Paine's representation of Wolfe's "removal" in the final stanza reinforces this reading. The fact that Wolfe pines to "hear" his victory is not simply Paine's nod to the extant ballads written in the wake of Wolfe's death, but a distinct and different response to Britannia's own sculpting of images into walls and dust.[24] Hearing here assures permanence and authenticity in a way Britannia could not with her testamentary acts; hearing signals vic-tory for Wolfe while sculpture signifies loss for Britannia, a significant shift from Wolfe pastorals and odes that made such hearing the maudlin irony of Wolfe's death.[25] As well, in contrast to the Wolfe portrayed in contemporary ballads and poems, Wolfe's hearing here is not a plaintive last moment but that which approves his death and the worth of his sacrifice. His "hearing" marks him not as the sentimental proto-romantic hero, nobly dying for Britain on a distant plain, but the autonomous agent of his own destiny. Wolfe will "obey," but only after the conditions he sets are met, and only after he fulfills earthly and earth-bound responsibility.

The limits of that obedience are the bounds within which Wolfe expresses a kind of patriotism that Paine sees as the consequence of Wolfe's death. The "fondness he bore to his own native shore" is simultaneously the quality that renders him attractive to the gods and that which repels him from his duty. And while this would seem to draw Wolfe back, and thus closer to Britannia, I would argue that given the increasing distance between Wolfe and Britannia over the course of the poem, Paine's phrasing is necessarily exact. Mercury's fear of Wolfe's attachment to his "native shore" necessitates a strange inurnment, and suggests that what draws Wolfe back is not his love for, or his attachment to, Britannia as embodied in an exalted object, as "a love of the green and pleasant homeland" England was often portrayed as in patriotic poetry.[26] This is a mere "shore," something distinct from the figure of Britannia in the poem but also, like "hearing" and "dust," something liminal and littoral, dividing and defining realms and spaces without entirely occupying any, and in contrast to the opening stanza's "mouldering cave," with its evocation of natural and inevitable decay. Indeed, the attraction of the shore is the impulse of the entire poem, the fable's work of shifting political definitions away from structures, institutions, and female-figured nations and onto individuals. "Native shore" is England-as-nature, not romanticized but simply extant, and Britannia is a personified institution. If the poem then chronicles the gradual yet inevitable separation of Wolfe from Britannia, there runs in parallel a move of all political authority and its vesting originary power from earth to heaven, from human to divine, to the native shore and away from Britannia.

And that, in the end, is why Wolfe can only be both "inurned" and "induced." "The funerary urn stood for death, that paradoxically sad and happy instant separating the mortal from the immortal soul," but Paine's Wolfe is inurned because rather than engravings in the dust, and Britannia's characteristically failed memorializing of that separation, Wolfe embodies his disembodiment, a living exemplum of the true price of the political life.[27] He is induced because inducement presupposes a kind of obscured logic presented to Wolfe in order to return, but also because such a motive for return is highly questionable. In the few times, three total, that Paine uses "induce" in his early political prose, the context is nearly always one of manipulation and trickery, and the same holds here in his poetry.[28] Any inducement to return to the native shore would, it seems, be rooted in an unethical and deceptive attempt at drawing Wolfe back into the orbit of Britannia and her dusty encomiums to what Wolfe represents to her needs, rather than what he stands for as an individual with the seed and source of political power. In that lies nothing less than the basic liberty that preoccupied Paine for the rest of his life.

THREE

The Shifted Vision

James Thomson and *Common Sense*

All his ideas, sentiments and versification seem peculiarly his own. There is beautiful wildness in his numbers, unpolished as they sometimes are; a manliness and majesty in his language, a decorum and spirit in his images, and a likeness in most of his descriptions, singularly new, inimitable and striking. And what of all others is perhaps the most decisive mark of a poetical mind, the objects he describes, though frequently common and familiar, strike us some how in a new light.

—John More, *Strictures, Critical and Sentimental, on Thomson's Seasons*

Written in 1777, only a year after Paine published *Common Sense,* but almost thirty years after the last edition of James Thomson's *Seasons,* John More's insights into the "poetical mind" of Thomson could just as insightfully refer to Paine's seminal pamphlet. The critical heritage on *Common Sense* is wide and deep and therefore nothing less than a Rorschach test for any scholar wishing to understand or comment on Paine's personality, political views, or rhetorical skills. And yet no scholarly assessment of *Common Sense* has seriously acknowledged the fact that on the pamphlet's title page, Paine included a quote from one of the most prominent and popular English poets of the eighteenth-century, the man whom More celebrates for his poetical decisiveness: James Thomson. Paine quotes a couplet from Thomson's *Liberty,* a poem "which enjoyed a fairly long gestation" and was published in five parts between 1735 and 1736 at the height of Thomson's immersion into Whig politics and the "patriot opposition" against Robert Walpole's administration.[1] Drawn specifically from "Britain," the fourth part of Thomson's long poem *Liberty,* the lines read, "Man knows no

Master save creating HEAVEN,/Or those whom choice and common good ordain" (636–37). As I intend to argue, the lines in particular, and the poem in general, are important references and persuasive imaginative frameworks for analyzing the arguments and rhetoric of *Common Sense,* as well as Paine's deliberate attempts at divesting Americans from the view that "most writers and readers in America considered themselves to be members of the generic English culture that we generally mean by 'British Culture.'"² Paine's mind, no less than Thomson's, is "poetic" because in quoting Thomson's poem he invokes Thomson's own poetic images, themes, arguments, and techniques from *Liberty;* in quoting the poet's name, Paine references and places his work alongside and astride the politics of patriot opposition that flourished in the 1730s and 1740s and that movement's deeply held belief that "patriotism was civic virtue, an ideal of selfless public activity."³ Bernard Bailyn suggests that *Common Sense* is "an English pamphlet written on an American theme," and the quotation of Thomson complicates this reading.⁴ By paratextually quoting and invoking the patriot opposition to Walpole, Paine offers *Common Sense* not merely as belated, but as the definitive extension, natural evolution, and logical political conclusion of that movement's ideology—a novel and necessary development of their politics and nothing else than an unequivocally American entry into the British discourse of patriotism that raged over much of the eighteenth century.

While a number of studies have examined the publication battles over early editions of *Common Sense,* the bibliographic evidence, battlefield residue of those battles, reveals that the quotation was a permanent and integral paratextual element on the title page.⁵ Richard Gimbel's exhaustive study of *Common Sense*'s bibliographical history shows that in both the first Robert Bell edition (January 1776) and the first Bradford edition (February 1776), published just weeks apart, the Thomson quote remained in place, and Bell continued to include it in his unauthorized, pirated editions after Paine had handed publication to the Bradfords. Bell also included the quotation in his initial newspaper advertisement to *Common Sense,* printed in the January 9, 1776, edition of the *Pennsylvania Evening Post,* and in additional advertisements in newspapers throughout the month of January. He likewise included the Thomson quotation in the full page advertisement for a "new" edition of *Common Sense* that he was publishing at the same time the Bradfords were publishing their authorized editions.⁶ It might be suggested that, at least in Bell's case, with the title page already set from his own first edition, it merely behooved him to keep the title page's form and forme in his subsequent editions, and to some extent his extensive use of the quotation in the newspaper debates over *Common Sense*'s publication suggest Bell saw it as part of his rightful control over the pamphlet. However, as Gimbel demonstrates, even an early German edition of *Common Sense* printed in Philadelphia in 1776 included the quotation, translated into German by the printers Cist and Steiner.[7]

Perhaps the most compelling evidence for the central role Thomson and *Liberty* play in *Common Sense* is offered by the most prominent response to it. Published by Robert Bell on March 13, 1776, and written by James Chalmers under the pseudonym Candidus as the "first response to Paine's massively popular pamphlet," *Plain Truth; Addressed to the Inhabitants of America, Containing, Remarks on a Late Pamphlet, Entitled Common Sense* rejoined Paine's call for independence and stood as "the most important American expression of the views of those whom Paine had so violently attacked—and the only American expression of those views known to Englishmen."[8] As Paine himself wrote of it, "the performance was too weak to do any hurt or deserve any answer."[9] Yet the real value of *Plain Truth* is not merely its failure, but the fact that in his response, Chalmers too chose to quote Thomson and *Liberty* on his title page. Gerard Genette has famously defined paratext as that which "constitutes a zone between text and off-text, a zone not only of transition but also *transaction:* a privileged place of a pragmatics and a strategy, of an influence on the public, an influence that . . . is at the service of a better reception for the text and a more pertinent reading of it." Chalmers's own quotation of Thomson suggests that both he and Paine saw their title pages as essential paratextual spaces and idealized places for the transactional nature of interpretation and "strategy" in the political contest for reconciliation or independence.[10] Part of that strategy is to shape a priori interpretive outcomes, since "for the reader, the relationship between introductory epigraph and text is still prospective," and an epigraph on a title page is especially so. Chalmers's title page is especially busy, containing an unattributed quote, "Will ye turn from flattery and attend this side?," and two lines from part 1 of *Liberty,* "Ancient and Modern Rome": "There TRUTH *unlicens'd,* walks, and dares accost / Even Kings themselves, the Monarchs of the Free!" (364–65).

Taking Paine's sentimental appeals in *Common Sense* as mere "flattery," Chalmers's use of the Thomson quote from the poem's first book rather than its fourth, wherein Thomson sees the ruins of modern Rome and considers the ancient ones upon which they are built, is a stark and emphatic claim on the side of American reconciliation with Great Britain and Chalmers's argument for the proper duty and purview of liberty. The figure of Liberty gazes upon Truth as it walks along Britain's shores, and the opening line turns upon two linked terms: "unlicens'd" and "accost." Such accosting is "daring" and conveys a sense of unwelcome hostility as well as approach and accompaniment, thereby making Truth the aggressive reality of kings, but also their equal. "Unlicens'd" then becomes the more powerful inducement to kings. Initially suggesting a lack of specifically documentary or chartered authority, Truth seems to "accost," in either sense, on no legitimate basis. It walks, but literally has no ground on which to do so. Yet since such truth accosts "even" monarchs of the "free," such "unlicensed" truth accrues to itself the sense not so much of undocumented authority but a quality and truth that parses and metes out liberty in perfectly just amounts, since license could mean "excessive liberty."[11] In this way, "unlicensed" and "free" at the start and end of the couplet are deeply related notions for Chalmers in his argument for reconciliation. Truth has a value in a British society ruled by monarchs specifically because they are the monarchs of the free, and such freedom, as much as the king's relation to it, is defined by a document: the English constitution. While truth's authority may be undocumented and unchartered, then, it nonetheless regulates the exercise and limits of liberty and complements the freedom under which kings rule and truth operates, because both exist only under the documentary guarantees of the English constitution and the government structures that operate for it.

That Chalmers understood the transactional nature of Paine's epigraph suggests Paine's was a provocative call for a distinctive and deliberate interpretive framework for *Common Sense*.[12] Indeed, in light of how Chalmers and *Plain Truth* used Thomson and "Liberty," Paine's own couplet choice is interesting for how it attempts to immediately foreground two basic aspects of *Common Sense:* the individual's freedom from monarchs, even of the free, and the basic choices confronting his readers, if not their consequences. Momentarily isolated from its larger context within part 4 of *Liberty,* and indeed by Paine not even indicated by its title, the line hints at Paine's deism and scaffolds his argument around three linked ideas. This much the Chalmers and Paine quotation share: they are each couplets whose poetic force lies in Thomson's special ability to enable the meaning of those couplets through related but not identical terms. The master man "knows" is primarily the continuous power of heaven, a metonym that asserts the power of God without naming one, a power without a personality. The subsequent line, on the force of the "Or" that opens it, ostensibly presents the neutral "those" as the subsequent candidate for man's "master," with "choice" and "common good" as legitimate alternatives to "creating heaven," since they seem to be distinct from heavenly powers. "Choice" is private, individual action while "common good" is the object of public virtue. Yet the force of the opening conjunction in Thomson's second line, as well as the neutral, unattached "those" compared to the very specific and defined concepts of "creating heaven," "choice," and "common good," is counterpoised by the enjambed alliterative connection between the three candidates for man's mastery: creating heaven, choice, and common good. Tied as they are by their *c* sounds, the terms are not so much distinct, alternative choices as a continuum of options related by the fact that they are all and each "ordained."

Paine's acute ear for Thomson's poetry shines through here. The immediate sense of "ordain," especially as the terminal word of the second line, links directly back to "heaven," the last word of the first line. Heaven's creating power persists throughout the couplet as that which, in one way or another, controls the ultimate outcome of man's master. The line is deist enough for Paine, and for the role God plays in *Common Sense*, but that is ultimately beside the point. The full verbal force of "ordain" lies in its secular meaning of "arrange, plan, or govern."[13] The grammatical emphasis of the second line offers the preferred ordinands as "choice" and "common good," meaning that it is representative, democratic political choice and the common public good that choice serves that rightly and inevitably tend to order "those" who are chosen. Yet the poetic meaning of "ordain" is precisely where man's power genuinely lies, namely the correct ordering of the three alliteratively linked ideas: the order of creating heaven, whose power constantly makes; the choice that is at the heart of Paine's argument for democratic government and against hereditary monarchies; and finally the common good that is the very subject and object of Paine's call for independence and the only legitimate result of using common sense. The interstitial space between those three ideals is for Paine the very heart of liberty.

While I have looked at the lines above in a kind of necessary isolation, and one which Paine encourages, it is the immediate, larger poetic context of part 4 of *Liberty* that Paine likewise directs his reader to consider. The poem opens with Liberty's romp through mediaeval Europe and its Northern regions. She then tarries in Italy where "Thrice happy they! / Had social *Freedom* bound their Peace, and Arts" (269–70). That social freedom, so vitally important for Thomson in the thriving of his liberty, and the guarantee of which is the very purpose of government, is precisely what Liberty finds when she consequently makes her way to Britain's shore:

Here, with the *shifted Vision* burst my Joy.
O the dear Prospect! O majestic View!
See BRITAIN's Empire! Lo! the watry Vast
Wide-waves, diffusing the Cerulean Plain. (381–84)

This characteristic "vision" of the progress poem is crucial, referring both
to the shift of Liberty's vision westward and northward from Italy to
Britain and also to "shift" in the sense of an "ingenious device for effecting
change; an expedient." Here the vision is an expedient for its very object,
namely Britain, but also serves in the progress poem as that which actualizes
much of what the poem's objects are, granting moral necessity to much of
what it offers for view.[14] This "attend[ing] to objects at a middle distance,
not (again) as points on a grid but as features of an ecology that change with
the position from which they are held" is precisely how Liberty will present
her virtues.[15]

Those virtues are subsequently described by Liberty. First Courage
("THAT VIRTUE known/By the relenting Look, whose equal Heart/For
Others feels, as for another Self," 486–87), then Justice ("The mother of
the state," 507), Sincerity, ("His pure untroubled Eye/The Fount of Truth,"
518–19), and next the paired virtues of Retirement and Independance. While
Retirement points to "that simple Life, the quiet-whispering Grove,/And
the still Raptures of the free-born Soul" (530–31), it is Independance, "to the
Public Scene/Demanded," that

> quit[s] his *sylvan Friend* a while;
> Nought can his Firmness shake, nothing seduce
> His Zeal, still active for the Common-Weal. (535–38)

While for Thomson Independance is a private sensibility that shares with
retirement the benefits of the private sphere, the inevitable draw (back) to
the "public scene" means it is likewise, if not more crucially, a public virtue,
and more properly exercised in the public sphere than enjoyed in the private. Note that while Retirement is characterized as having and producing
"still raptures," Independance is "still active for the Common-Weal." If Retirement is "still"—quiet, unproductive, and passive—then Independance
is "still": continuously "active" within the public sphere because it best
operates within and is defined by it.

After noting that Independance "greatly scorns" (543) "stormy *Tyrants*"
and "Corruption's Tools" (539), as well as those "foul ministers" (540) who

accept "shameful honours" and "perfidious gifts" (542), Thomson claims that "if he must betray/His plunder'd Country, or his Power resign,/A Moment's Parley were eternal Shame" (543–45). That noble sacrifice in the public sphere, for the common, public good answers shame with a retreat to the private, a kind of cover for Independance's detachment from the conventional markers of public recognition, since

> Illustrious into private Life again,
> From dirty *Levees* he unstain'd ascends
> And firm in Senates stands the *Patriot's* ground,
> Or draws new Vigour in the peaceful Shade. (546–49)

Given the poetic hectoring of the lines describing Independance, filled with multiple enjambments and charting Independance's dizzy move from private retirement to deployment in the public sphere and back to a "vigourous" private life embodied by the privileged poetic shade, Independance remains as the single virtue that bridges the public and private divide, and is subsequently embodied in the language of land. The "dirty levees" are at once raised earthen mounds whose heights are ultimately overshadowed by Independance's "ascension" above them and simultaneously desecrated public ceremonies. The essentially fluid, oscillating imagery functions as the imaginative equivalent of the multiple enjambed lines, as well as the counterpoint to Thomson's insistence that where his shifted vision rests is emphatically, singularly, "here." While Independance ascends, it does so only to stand "firm" on the necessarily elevated "patriot's ground," and Independance has to go up to go down. That Independance stands "firm" harkens back a mere (if symmetrical) ten lines previous to the recognition that "nought can his firmness shake," and it is no coincidence that such "firmness"—a quality of good ground it should be noted—is the segue at each stanzaic point of Independance's passage between public and private life. Such firmness equally means that the "or" which opens the final line ("Or draws new vigour in the peaceful shade") has the same deceptively simple conjunctive function as that last line of Paine's epigraphical quotation, proposing as it ostensibly does that standing firm in senate and holding the "patriot's ground" is somehow equivalent, or merely alternative, to the "vigour" of the shade. Instead, while Independance both begins and ends in the private sphere, the entire heft of the lines, and where their enjambed and dizzying journey leads, is to the necessarily public character of Independance as a virtue, but likewise to its entrenched value as something that never leaves the public sphere in an uncomplicated or merely equal exchange for the private life and retirement.

After the poem catalogues a number of other native British virtues, there is another characteristic "shift" in Liberty's vision ("Now turn your view," 623) from the description of native British virtues to the history of Liberty in Britain, which begins with "mark[ing] from *Celtic* Night/To present Grandeur how my BRITAIN rose" (624–25). Such "grandeur" begins with the Druids, "commandeered by the emergent Patriot movement,"[16] who

> taught, that Death but shifts
> The vital Scene, . . . that prime Fear despis'd;
> And, prone to rush on Steel, disdain'd to spare
> An ill-sav'd Life that must again return. (630–33)

Another crucial "shift" occurs here as the Druids' "belief in spiritual transmigration encouraged the early Britons the more readily to sacrifice their lives in resistance to Roman tyranny."[17] Indeed, such a belief fosters in the Druids a very particular nature:

> Erect from *Nature's* Hand, by *tyrant Force*,
> And still more *tyrant Custom*, unsubdu'd,
> Man knows no Master save creating HEAVEN,
> Or such as Choice and Common Good ordain.
> This general Sense, with which the Nations I
> Promiscuous fire, in BRITONS burn'd intense,
> Of future Times prophetic. (634–40)

Paine's chosen quotation gains measurably by its immediate poetic context, and it is perhaps unremarkable that the language of the Druidical sacrifice is nearly identical to Thomson's own language of liberty. Not only does the Druidical belief in the mere "shift" between life and death echo the monumental shift of Liberty's vision to Britain, but the fact that it is "still" more tyrant custom invokes such custom, and especially resistance to it, "dispair'd" and "disdain'd," as a necessary condition for the fruition of independence. That connection between tyrant custom and independence will be utterly vital for Paine in *Common Sense*.

In a grammatically difficult line, the "general Sense" that the Druids awaken with their willing sacrifice and freedom to "ordain" their own masters is "fire[d]" by Liberty, but once again it is the enjambed structure of the two lines that complicates. The immediate reading seems to place promiscuity as a description of the firing; its diffusiveness will readily spread both out among the Britons and down through British history. Yet the grammar of the lines and the odd visual and grammatical isolation of the "I" at the end of the line points to Liberty describing herself as promiscuous, and therefore promiscuous to one end: the prophecy of "future Times." This, then, is another of the Thomsonian themes Paine will bring to *Common Sense*, namely the sense that what both independence and the rejection of "tyrant custom" ultimately shape is not simply the character of those who practice them, or even the very liberty that both guarantees and is won by them. Rather, it is the longitudinal, proleptic impact and influence of those qualities, which are both beholden to the time but likewise shape it and fashion it, that will be an important part of Paine's arguments in *Common Sense*, since, as he states in his introduction, "A long habit of not thinking a thing *wrong*, gives it a superficial appearance of being *right*, and raises at first a formidable outcry in defence of custom. But the tumult soon subsides. Time makes more converts than reason."[18]

Thomson and *Liberty* are then pervasive influences on *Common Sense*. Paine's opening, "On The Origin and Design of Government in General, With Concise Remarks on the English Constitution," offers his well-known definition of government as "even in its best state, . . . but a necessary evil . . . government, like dress, is the badge of lost innocence." "Security," Paine argues, is the "true design and end of government." And to demonstrate this very end, Paine narrates a mini-history of society and liberty: "Let us suppose a small number of persons settled in some sequestered part of the earth. . . . Necessity, like a gravitating power, would soon form our newly arrived emigrants into society . . . and render the obligations of law and government unnecessary while they remained perfectly just to each other." Yet soon, "they will begin to relax in their duty and attachment to each other: and this remissness will point out the necessity of establishing some form of government to supply the defect of moral virtue." Subsequently "some convenient tree will afford them a State House, under the branches of which the whole colony may assemble to deliberate on public matters," which quickly turns into a representative assembly as the colony grows and disperses in size and population, thus creating a constant interchange between the electors and the elected, and "this frequent interchange will establish a common interest with every part of the community . . . and on this, (not on the unmeaning name of king,) depends the *strength of government, and the happiness of the governed*."[19]

Like Thomson in *Liberty*, Paine adapts the skeletal outlines of the progress poem's poetic form in order to both justify and describe his vision of government.[20] As Robin Dix has pointed out, the progress poem moves through various stages and "accentuates [a] motif of individual and social development" through each stage, while R. H. Griffith has pithily defined the genre as "an imaginary tour of an allegorical abstraction" in which the particular strain of history and politics "passes from . . . a pageant of independent, unconnected scenes to . . . a pageant dominated by a principle of continuity."[21] Thomson's *Liberty* is a "failed" progress, and while that failure is as alluring to Paine as the structure of progress, Paine's opening gambit must be read as a kind of progress poem in prose that forsakes allegory for the continuity of the history of government. His "small number of persons" who form the basic unit of society live in natural liberty and simple justice, but either because "the strength of one man is so unequal to his wants" or "his mind so unfitted for perpetual solitude," he is "soon obliged to seek assistance and relief of another, who in his turn requires the same."[22] Although initially "perfectly just" to one another, these people will soon reveal the "defect" in moral virtue that leads them to government. That government in turn will begin simply but grow not more complicated but more complex, as both the social structure of government progresses and the individual roles of people develop from mere members of society to the specified roles of electors and elected. What began as isolation and loneliness progresses to not merely society but frequent, creative "interchange," "common interest," and "community." There is a distinctive continuity here, as even the "defect in moral virtue" that necessitates the translation from society to government is read neither as a preponderant burden nor a thing to be regretted. Rather, from their localized natural liberty and perfect justice, to their continental legislature that both represents society in government and begins to differentiate individual roles within that society through government, there is a linear progression where each transition is read as a continuity that finds its greatest expression in the interplay of interchange, common interest, and community.[23]

What distinguishes *Liberty* as a progress poem is, of course, its emphasis on vision as the privileged instrument and very sensory organ of progress itself. Indeed, vision does not have an uncomplicated history in Thomson studies, and Paine adapts a distinct visionary aspect for his own mini-progress: "And however our eyes may be dazzled with show, or our ears deceived by sound; however prejudice may warp our wills, or interest darken our understanding, the simple voice of nature and reason will say, 'tis right."[24] By first warning that "our eyes may be dazzled by show," Paine is engaging in a distinctly Thomsonian quality of vision, namely the consideration of "perceiving [as] an active process—more on the pattern of touch than vision—and [a model] that proposes that what the senses do is make the world available rather than hold it at a skeptical remove."[25] Paine's vision is both "active process" and poetic progress; Paine's vision of natural simplicity magnifies that tactile availability of both the world and the truth of it, and the competing alternative, namely monarchies and their rituals of power, dampens and distances the senses, specifically vision, and availability. It "dazzles," thereby overwhelming by complex, multiple stimuli the vision that for Paine is and ought to be "simple." That is the prior and necessary vision to the subsequent cascade of failures: the deception of sound and the warping of wills by prejudice, which becomes Paine's shorthand for Thomson's "tyrant custom" throughout *Common Sense* and here is asserted as the consequence of a distorted vision, as much as the "interest" that darkens understanding. Thus, not simply are Thomson's major structural and thematic elements pervasive here, but the prevailing notion concerning the utter centrality of vision abides, as does its role in making the new political world described by Paine accessible and therefore democratic.

That is why the rest of the first part of *Common Sense* treats the English constitution and the reasons it depends not on the king but on the "republican" House of Commons, and why the second section treats the biblical history of monarchy. This is a digressive history, and Paine's recounting of how the Israelites chose their kings largely out of ignorance and despite the best recommendations of their scriptures serves as the best justification for his choice of epigraph. Paine then moves on to the third part, "Thoughts on the Present State of American Affairs." He almost immediately begins by picking up the thread directly from the "dazzle" passage of the first section: "In the following pages I offer nothing more than simple facts, plain arguments, and common sense: and have no other preliminaries to settle with the reader, than that he will divest himself of prejudice and pre-possession, and suffer his reason and his feelings to determine for themselves: that he will put on, or rather that he will not put off, the true character of a man, and generously enlarge his views beyond the present day."[26] Martin Roth has written of this passage that "the conditions that Paine demands for the reading of his intimidating and seductive rhetoric are themselves the transformation he projects," and such transformation is distinctly Thomsonian in argument and style.[27] That in-born druidical repulsion to "tyrant custom" is here embedded in the negative call for character. What neither Paine, nor Liberty, nor Independence offer is the chance to create anew the character with the very "power of feelings" Paine claims at the end of his introduction to *Common Sense;* instead Paine asks that the reader "not put off" what is already essential to his character. The druidical appeal as the "mythical . . .

leaders of British resistance to Roman tyranny" is, immediately after George III is called a "ruffian," made specifically American, as the unshakably native character to which all Americans are bound. Likewise, "tyrant custom" is here rendered as "prejudice," which Paine uses throughout *Common Sense* "to spur [his readers] into epistemological reflection, in other words, to think about the ways in which they have been perceiving the world."[28] Such perception, of course, is precisely the function of vision in Thomson and in Paine, and why the mechanism to shift perception is "enlarging" in the "present day." Enlarging tends to obviate dazzlement; such enlargement within and necessarily beyond the "present" day makes it no less than Thomson's a vision of "future Times prophetic."

Paine takes up these themes two paragraphs later, in what is simply his most evocative, imaginative passage:

> The sun never shone on a cause of greater worth. 'Tis not the affair of a city, a county, a province, or a kingdom; but of a continent—of at least one eighth part of the habitable globe. 'Tis not the concern of a day, a year, or an age; posterity are virtually involved in the contest, and will be more or less affected even to the end of time, by the proceedings now. Now is the seed-time of continental union, faith and honor. The least fracture now will be like a name engraved with the point of a pin on the tender rind of a young oak; the wound would enlarge with the tree, and posterity read it in full grown characters.[29]

Bursting with the natural imagery of suns, seeds, globes, and oaks, the passage is framed by Paine's own elaborative version of the "future times" prophesied, which he, no less than liberty, is trying to promiscuously fire. The imaginary movement from the sun to the globe moves through a kind of oscillating sequence that is structurally reminiscent of Thomson's own description of Independance. Paine moves up to the sun, then down to the city through to the continent and out to the whole globe, itself encompassed by the necessity of the "cause," which serves to "counter the feared scene of postcolonial disintegration with one of monumental U.S. integrity."[30] This, then, is an ecology of Paine's vision, "using his own craft to show how objects are made present to whoever beholds them."[31] Here though, it is not "firmness" that frames the movements of the passage. It is "posterity," personified as those who are "virtually" involved, and Paine's use of "posterity" is ingenious in its personification, a kind of after-effect of the progress-poem beginning of *Common Sense*, and in its visionary ecological relationship to the three instances of "now" in the passage: "the pamphlet also derives its power from its ability to personalize the future in such a way as to transform the future from an abstract concept into a concrete reality."[32] Immediately paired together in a kind of double-shot—"by the proceedings now. Now is the seed-time"—and completed later in "the least fracture now," the tripartite deployment places an absolute insistence on the present moment as the essential one for the as yet in the text unnamed "proceedings." The genuine moral and political imperative of the "now" is precisely what posterity will do with and in it: "read the engraving in full grown characters." The chronological movement of time and in time as the young oak grows old returns to Paine's progress-poem-structured opening. Having "heard" the voice of nature and reason in the first part of *Common Sense*, now they—personified posterity—can read; now they use their vision, having exactly the tactile sensibility that presents the world to posterity as it is, not at a remove but in the form of engraving and fully grown characters. "Engraving" is a vital poetic image for Paine and here it is no less so, a function of Paine's Thomsonian vision because such engraving happens upon a popular symbol for British royalty and naval might, traditionally a symbol of the "myth" of British power but likewise a "contested symbol" used by both Jacobites and Whigs as symbols of their respective political beliefs.[33] Thomson was not beyond "politicizing the oak" in his masque *Britannia*, but the strong connections of the oak to British politics suggest that Paine's act, and that of his "American-to-be" posterity, personified as the end of progress, is one of engraving, as it was for "The Death of General Wolfe," as a fundamentally transgressive act. It may be that Paine's is a "process of rational deconstruction . . . offered as a mode of revolution," but it is equally a progress of visionary deconstruction, etched in the oak as America's own revolutionary act in time and for posterity as inheritors of the prophesied future times.[34]

The imaginative work of this paragraph keenly reflects Paine's poetic sensibilities in *Common Sense*, so much so that what John More says of Thomson could apply to Paine's imagery: "One principle purpose of true poetry, is to heighten [the] mental harmony, and by uttering the ideas of the understanding, in perfect consonance with the feelings of the heart, to abate the prevailing asperity of our natures and improve our habits of sympathy."[35] As Paine moves through the third section of *Common Sense*, that habit of sympathy built upon the earlier passage becomes a central focus: "But let our imaginations transport us a few moments to Boston, that seat of wretchedness will teach us wisdom; and instruct us for ever to renounce a power in whom we can have no trust." Trish Loughran suggests,

"Paine's version of 'transport' relies . . . on something more like interior enlightenment—the sort of 'transport' that turns on a powerful leap of the mind. Even so, *Common Sense* almost always insists that such inner epiphanies turn on an appeal to the local, the embodied." As an example, she insists that Paine's claim "our affections are wounded by the pores" is "punningly evoking, with the word 'pore,' the American ports at the center of colonial trade disputes."[36] That is something of a stretch; what explains the pores is that in his argument for "imaginative transportation" it is not so much transportation which is key but imagination, since "the nature of the poetic enterprise makes imagining more important."[37] The focus of drawing affections out of the microscopic detail of facial pores bears a poetic specificity that is Thomsonian in nature and degree, since "Thomson varies the principle of realizing the invisible," and by so doing, achieves his "underlying aim to communicate complex (spatial, temporal, emotional) meanings simultaneously. Some of these entail the construction of images of growth, mobility, and extension that are followed by moments of accomplishments, stasis, or death."[38] While not invisible, the pores are so microscopically small that they effectively are, and by evoking and promiscuously firing his readers' imaginations Paine generates a Thomsonian poetic and imaginary effect to spur their affections, and most importantly to lead them to consider not simply "the possibility of a world revolution played out in innumerable local sites" but that "government of our own is our natural right."[39] Only within those habits of sympathy, and by generating consonances between ideas and heart, can Paine make that claim to the natural right of government. The key is that only through the poetic nature of his imagery, and the specifically Thomsonian nature of that imagery, could Paine make that claim. Only by creating an image of imaginative mobility could Paine and his readers conclude that feeling affections at the pore could lead to the ultimate accomplishment: both natural rights and natural rights to government.

The fourth section of *Common Sense* moves away from the imaginative. This tonal shift late in the text to more practical and less visionary and imaginative matters may seem jarring at first, but the talk about debt, and the virtues of accruing debt in order to fund a navy that could rival England's, is not so much a matter of the practical measures needed to secure independence for the colonies as it is Paine securing the claims for an American patriotism that is equal parts commercial and political, skirting but deliberately not addressing the worries that luxury and commerce were actually corroding influences on all potential expressions of political virtue.[40] Indeed, such an argument was essential to Thomson. Dustin Griffin points out that

"Thomson's celebration of Britain's trading empire is calculated to assuage the concerns of moralists who worried about the corrupting effect of luxury" by arguing that Britain's world empire was "cause for patriotic pride, as was the naval power that opened the sea lanes and maintained British control of them."[41] Paine's calculation for an American navy, including the willingness to incur a national debt, is nothing less than Paine's American appropriation of Thomson's poetic rationale for British power and the basis for British patriotism. For Paine, a singular kind of American patriotism will be rooted in support of the navy because it will protect the interests of America as the English never could. That is why the fourth part ends with the claim, "These proceedings may at first seem strange and difficult, but like all other steps which we have already passed over, will in a little time become familiar and agreeable: and until an independence is declared, the continent will feel itself like a man who continues putting off some unpleasant business from day to day, yet knows it must be done, hates to set about it, wishes it over, and is continually haunted with the thoughts of its necessity."[42] Such an image of trepidation and paralyzing tarrying is the figure of the anti-patriot, of those who given both the time and the opportunity, are catatonically unable to act in ways that support the state, or perhaps more importantly, whose stasis and paralysis is the inverse simulacrum of the very "independance" and firmness Thomson has offered as British patriotic virtue. Paine has radically and necessarily transformed Thomson's "independance" from the largely patriotic and public but essentially private virtue that compels public service into a moral and political necessity justified by anger and the simple, natural rights of Americans.

This, then, is why Paine's persistent evocation of Thomson situates *Common Sense* as a belated response to what Dustin Griffin characterizes as the discourse of patriotism in the eighteenth century. A concept defined by a loosely assembled group of writers and politicians, largely Whig in belief, it was subsumed under an umbrella that included nationalism, claims to English liberty, and disputes over perceived tyrannical extensions of monarchical power. Ed Larkin has noted the ghost of Bolingbroke that hangs over *Common Sense*, specifically in the call for simple, and thus limited, government by natural right, and by quoting Thomson on the title page, Paine deliberately evokes the period in which these patriot disputes were waged. As well, in keeping with his acceptance of the prophesied future times as one of the governing motifs of *Common Sense*, Paine suggests that what his pamphlet represents is the natural and necessary evolution of these arguments into American terms. It is democracy and representative government, not mixed government, that assures the liberty of the people and healthy economic policies. It is not a king but elected representatives who through "interchange" effect the changes necessary to ensure freedom and security. It is not the exalted, imaginary English constitution or the reforms of 1688 that guarantee those liberties, nor is it even that tradition and the past into which one must look for rights. It is to nature and natural rights that one must look; it is the future, to posterity, for posterity, and to the everlasting now to which liberty is owed, and together nature and the future are the firm ground upon which patriotism and independence are planted. Samuel Johnson's famous definition of a patriot ("One whose ruling passion is the love of his country. It is sometimes used for a factious disturber of the government") is meant to be an ironic challenge to the very discourse of patriotism addressed in *Common Sense,* but for Paine, and the American patriotism he therein offers, Johnson's ironically oppositional terms genuinely are synonymous.[43] This synonymity, then, is the real patriotic import and impact of Paine's famous dictum that "we have it in our power to begin the world over again." That is nothing less than American liberty's promiscuous fire, its best patriotic expression, and the content of its own prophesied future.

If that power to begin again is an essential patriotic principle for Paine, then it must be acknowledged that perhaps the most important component of Paine's extension of Thomson's British patriotism was embedded and implicit within Thomson's poetry and the discourse of patriotism itself. Christine Gerrard has noted that one strand of the patriot ideology, as exemplified by Bolingbroke and his journal the *Craftsman,* was "a gloomy prognosis of Britain's imminent decline in a malaise of luxury and selfishness."[44] And in his final lines, Thomson acknowledges that gloominess:

As thick to View THESE VARIED WONDERS rose,
Shook all my Soul with Transport, unassur'd,
The VISION broke; And, on my waking Eye,
Rush'd the still RUINS of dejected ROME. (5:717–20)

As Suvir Kaul has written of these lines: "The poet's dynamic vision of British glory fragments into an awareness of the mutability of empires, and of the still ruins they leave behind. If *Liberty* is a monument to the dream of empire that so energized Thomson and his contemporaries, . . . it is also a reminder that this dream was far from seamless or consistent (or even comforting) and that it included many reminders of the costs and hesitation of overseas triumph."[45] Horribly isolated and hemmed in by two commas, and placed at the end of a poetic line as empty as Liberty's "I" in part 4, "unassur'd" refers to both the poet's "Transport" and the "vision." Behold Thomson's last bequeathal to Paine. As integral as his thematics, image making, and individual poetic style and structures were for *Common Sense,* and as much as Thomson's participation in the "patriot opposition" generated a vibrant and workable model of both patriotism and independence, what he, as a staunch supporter of a political system and monarch that Paine had necessarily to reject, finally gave Paine was the opening. A mere suggestion but not so mere a possibility: a doorway of doubt and a seed of skepticism about that very system, and a seminal uneasiness with the costs of its existence. The end result was that this doubt and skepticism rejected not only the notion of British empire but colonial American attachment to their British identity. Leonard Tennenhouse has argued: "For a colonist in America to declare himself a Briton was evidently to make a reasonable claim to national identity. Although they were called 'Americans,' that term did not in any way cancel out the more fundamental British identity that tied them to their nation of origin."[46] Yet Paine's epigraphic appropriation of Thomson's own political views in *Common Sense* both cancels out and renders highly unreasonable any colonial American claim to Britishness because of the American patriotism he persuasively promotes. That is why Paine can end his work on what has been called a "positive nationalism" in his own final lines: "Instead of gazing at each other with suspicions or doubtful curiosity, let each of us hold out to his neighbor the hearty hand of friendship, and unite in drawing a line, which, like an act of oblivion, shall bury in forgetfulness every former dissension."[47] If Liberty's vision was ultimately unsustainable, then Paine preempts that possibility. The patriot opposition had often called for the "burial of party labels," and Paine imagines that in both the creatively paradoxical dividing lines that unite and in the characterization of that drawing as an act of both oblivion and forgetting. This, then, is the culmination of time in Paine; this is what constitutes American liberty and patriotism and through each a politically independent America and necessarily coterminous American identity, based on a Thomsonian model where the lingering sense is that one's vision is constantly shifting. That, quite simply, was for Paine both common sense and plain truth.

FOUR

Pen and Soul; Glory and Nothing

Charles Churchill and *Crisis II*

The Glory and the Nothing of a Name.

—George Gordon, Lord Byron, "Churchill's Grave"

Byron's famous description of Charles Churchill's meteoric rise and fall in poetry during a brief period in the early 1760s acknowledges the difficulty of assessing his work beyond its vitriolic contempt for the ministry of Prime Minister John Stuart, 3rd Earl of Bute, and the reign of George III, or its exploration of what one scholar has called "the shifting, incongruous, contextual life of real human beings."[1] However, "contempt" and "incongruity" offer a compelling rationale for what readers of Paine's second *Crisis* paper (henceforth *Crisis II*) would find in January 1777: Churchill's name placed below the only epigraph in the entire series, a line taken and deliberately modified by Paine from Churchill's poem "The Author" (1763). The original reads, "What's in this name of *Lord,* that we should fear/To bring their vices to the public ear?" (157–58); Paine's epigraph offers, "What's in this name of Lord, that we should fear/To bring my grievance to the public ear?" Both the choice of verse and its emendation reflect Paine's concerns in *Crisis II* and its focus on the fearless role authors ought to play as public critics of political figures. The epigraph also reflects the deeply subjective, personal nature of the offence perpetrated by the particular public figures to whom the paper is dedicated: William and Richard Howe, brothers and commanders of British naval and land forces in America at the time of publication.

This deeply personal epigraphic configuration of Churchill and the Howe brothers standing as oppositional names on the title page, yet equally shifting signifiers for Paine's arguments and intentions in the paper, contributes

63

to *Crisis II*'s argument for a new revolutionary model of authorship, one that both shares and rejects the standard understanding of republican print ideology as something necessarily obliterating authorial personality in its elevation of print and printedness as markers of an emerging public sphere of reason and reasoned criticism of public institutions. Instead, by both adopting and adapting the terminology and thematics of his poetic epigraphic source, as well as other works to which the title *Crisis* refers, Paine seeks to assure the centrality of the authorial figure to American independence and that the Howe brothers, as contending personalities on the battlefield of revolutionary authorship, would share some of the nothingness, but not the glory, of Churchill's name.

The *Crisis* papers, a series of sixteen pamphlets written between December 1776 and April 1783, chronicle the vicissitudes of the revolutionary war as witnessed and experienced by Paine. Opening *Crisis I* with the famous statement "These are the times that try men's souls," Paine spent the essays ranging over a multitude of topics. The papers have been described as "perfectly timed and adapted to the needs of the time, . . . enormously aid[ing] the American cause and contribut[ing] to no small extent to ultimate victory," although of all his major early works, it is the *Crisis* papers that have received the least amount of critical attention.[2] Paine took his title from a series of English essays called *The Crisis*, written by an anonymous group of authors and published in London between January 1775 and October 1776. Unabashed in their criticism of British policy in America, written with invective language meant to "maximize [their] shock value, using a public forum to berate the king and rouse his subjects," and "to draw analogies between British and American conditions, to speak of the common cause, a transatlantic association of the aggrieved," the English *Crisis* papers never shied away from engaging in inflammatory rhetoric to evince their causes, even to the point of welcoming accusations of seditious libel.[3] This is reflected in their opening passage:

> To the people of England and America. Friends and fellow subjects: It is with the greatest Propriety I address this Paper to you. It is in your Defence, at that GREAT, this IMPORTANT CRISIS, I take the Pen in hand: A CRISIS big with the Fate of the most glorious Empire known in the Records of Time; and by *your* FIRMNESS and RESOLUTION ONLY, it can be saved from DESTRUCTION: By *your* FIRMNESS and RESOLUTION, you may preserve to yourselves, your immediate Offspring, and latest Posterity, all the glorious Blessings of FREEDOM,

given by *Heaven,* to undeserving mortals: By *your* SUPINENESS and PUSSILANIMITY, you will entail on yourselves, your Children, and *Millions* yet unborn, MISERY and SLAVERY.[4]

Often invoking the figure of John Wilkes and his campaign for civil liberties against the Earl of Bute and George III in the late 1750s and early 1760s as the paradigm for the American rejection of British tyranny by the very same king, the English *Crisis* papers, on a weekly basis between 1775 and 1776, framed the debate and the stakes of the American response not simply as a point of policy but as the necessary acts of a people who had already distinguished themselves from their colonial parent. They further framed separation as a necessary, compelled act performed in order to ensure the rejection of slavery and abjection and to defy George, his ministers, and his parliament. In short, separation was meant to purge and dispel the prevailing notion of the relationship between those three entities and the colonial policies that emerged from them.

Paine's paratextual evocation of Churchill and the English *Crisis* thus frames his own *Crisis* paper as a reiteration and repeat of Wilkes's (in)famous battle against Parliament and George III and the English *Crisis*'s boisterous attempts to awake the political sentiments of both the English and Americans to a common cause of freedom. This is nowhere more evident than in Paine's opening paragraph to *Crisis II:* "Universal empire is the prerogative of a writer. His concerns are with all mankind, and though he cannot command their obedience, he can assign them their duty. The Republic of Letters is more ancient than the monarchy, and of far higher character in the world than the vassal court of Britain; he that rebels against reason is a real rebel, but he that in defence of reason rebels against tyranny has a better title to *'Defender of the Faith,'* than George the Third."[5] On its surface, the paragraph announces most forcefully the well-known formulation of republican print ideology—as summarized by Michael Warner, "that print discourse was a cultural matrix in which the definitions of 'individual,' 'print,' 'public' and 'reason' were readjusted in a new set of ground rules for discourse. The politics of printed texts in republican America lay as much in the cultural meaning of their printedness as in their objectified nature or the content of their arguments."[6] That very republic, older and therefore of more authority and influence than George's court, in this passage advocates for and legitimizes the foremost agent of categorical and therefore cultural "readjustment": the writer. In "assigning duty," that writer makes reason not an exercise of the intellectual faculty as much as a political principle for independence and the rejection of monarchy as a political system. And yet the presence, and insistence upon, "prerogative" in that same passage actively resists such a reading, quite simply because it is a concept whose use in the passage is taken directly from both of Paine's paratextaully evoked sources: John Wilkes and Charles Churchill's radical newspaper the *North Briton* and the English *Crisis*.

The English *Crisis* had presented a largely salutary definition of prerogative in its twenty-fourth issue: "A Disease in the venal Majority in the great Council of the Nation, may be truly called a Mortification in the Body politic. This desperate Case requires a desperate Remedy. . . . The Operation of a wholesome and salutary Desolation has been wisely intrusted by our considerate Ancestors to the Sovereign. The Execution of this great Prerogative was petitioned for, with the greatest Reason, during the Tyranny and Iniquities of the last venal Parliament, by the first, the most loyal, and most respectable Metropolis in the Universe, the City of London."[7] Casting about both recent and ancient history to reiterate the prerogative of kings to shape parliaments, their behaviors, and their policies, the *Crisis* writers see prerogative as a hedge against the "tyrannies and iniquities" that arise in "venal" and thus bribable and illegitimate parliaments. The issue goes on to say, "This Prerogative (a glorious one it is) is intrusted with the Sovereign by the People, to be by him exerted in the nicest and most critical Emergencies of State," largely because "of all the Prerogatives of the Crown, the most essential to the Constitution, the most salutary to the People, the most Honourable to a Patriot King, is that of dissolving Parliaments. In this respect a King of England is wisely invested by the People with the Power of a temporary Dictator."[8] Both "intrusted" and "invested" to the king by the people, the potentially dangerous possibility of giving the King dictatorial power is legitimized only when it is given not just to the correct person but the correct *kind* of person: "The Truth is, that so glorious a Prerogative cannot be justly exercised, or wisely conducted, without a discerning Judgment, and a good Heart; without Fortitude sufficient to throw off the Leading strings of presumptuous Favourites, and Sense enough to proceed without them; without Capacity to think, and Ability to act . . . without adhering to Facts instead of Favourites; to Truth instead of ministerial Sophistry."[9] More than a defense of royal prerogative, the English *Crisis* presents a plea for the ideal conditions under which prerogative is exercised, and a curt reminder that rather than ministers and their sophistry, it is from the people that both the power and the authority of prerogative come. Prerogative is for the English *Crisis* at once a democratic principle and also a principle of authenticity, that which the people give to the king in order to authenticate his, and their own, political virtues. Surely, the passage is one of deep wish-fulfilment and proleptic fantasies on the nature of the English constitution, but Paine leverages its sense of prerogative perfectly for his own uses in the opening paragraph of *Crisis II.* His "universal empire" is not so much un-mitigated power as it is the privilege of the writer to opine on behalf of the people, and his "assigning of duty" is a responsibility that Paine undertakes both on behalf of, and at the behest of, the same people who grant kings their authority, or more precisely, who can and ought to reject that power as unreasonable. As will become evident as *Crisis II* continues, such pre-rogative working to create the Republic of Letters and bolster reason hinges almost entirely on the character of the writer—Paine—himself, no less so than the English *Crisis* thought for the king.

For Paine, however, this is no simple substitution. Instead, it is a cate-gorical addition to the King-Minister-Parliament-People dynamic at work in both the *North Briton* and the English *Crisis,* a necessary new position in the democratic revolution the Americans were fighting, and losing, at the time Paine was writing the paper. Indeed, as the English *Crisis* made clear, the uses of prerogative include the immediate and necessary obviation of ministerial conniving. That sense of prerogative as a weapon against minis-terial power plays was the only way the *North Briton* could ever understand prerogative: "If the giant *prerogative* is to be let loose, and stalk about, to create unusual terrors, and inflict unpractised punishments . . . we may then boast as much as we please, of our invaluable liberties, purchased with the blood of our heroic ancestors; but let us watch them narrowly, lest, before we are aware, they should soon depend upon too slight a thread."[10] For Wilkes and Churchill, it is not prerogative that is given over, it is liberties that have been given up. There is, however, "one consolation . . . that so se-vere an exercise of the *extreme right of the prerogative* cannot fail of recoiling soon upon the heads of those impetuous and rash minsters who first advised it. The chariot of the sun, which they have borrowed, will be theirs but for a day. They may, for a short time endanger our little world; but their own ruin will be the certain consequence. Their fall will be unpitied; their memories forever detested."[11] The *North Briton*'s version of prerogative is nightmarish, the last thing given over before the utter eradication of liberty; but the key difference between this and the English *Crisis* vision of prerogative is not so much their overall assessment of it but rather their agents. If the En-glish *Crisis* furnished a plea for the moderate and virtuous use of prerogative by a putatively virtuous king, then the *North Briton* understands that such prerogative is a function of ministerial, not royal, power, dictating a terror that will inevitably redound upon the heads of those who exercise it. And in that, prerogative takes on the nature of a "command," the very thing Paine rejects as the central action of his own authorial prerogative.

It is then these registers of prerogative, one dependent upon the strength of character, the other vitiated by those who exercise it in their ministerial roles, that Paine contends with in *Crisis II*, and they cohere around his self-emended poetic epigraph. While the original reads "bring their vices to the public ear" (158), Paine emends it to "bring my grievance to the public ear."[12] The change is vital to understanding Paine's intentions in the paper. Churchill's original places emphasis on the vicious nature and acts of the ministers; their public exposure is his promise, and their intimidation he flouts by claiming that he need not be afraid of what they may do or the power they have. Paine inverts this; it is not the vices of the ministers he wishes to publicize but the personal, subjective grievances he and all Americans suffer. The airing of those grievances will lead directly to the exposure of those ministerial vices. Paine thus invokes the necessity of character as a medium of public information but likewise the perfidious nature of the ministerial class who assert prerogative as an adjunct to fear and terror.

In this way Paine adopts Churchill's own poetic theme of "reflexivity and contradiction" as fundamental to *Crisis II*, especially as they play out in the poem from which Paine takes his epigraph, "The Author."[13] Known primarily for his scathing theatrical satires, especially "The Rosciad," or his poetry's "denunciations of mechanicalism, neutrality and rigidity, whether in business, literature, politics, or love," Churchill originally published "The Author" in 1763, offering a pessimistic overview of authorship in the perilous political times of his fame.[14] As the opening stanza reads:

> Accurs'd the man, whom fate ordains, in spite,
> And cruel parents teach, to Read and Write!
> What need of letters? Wherefore should we spell?
> Why write our names? A mark will do as well. (1–4)

Daniel Brewer's suggestion that Churchill's name "was used in ways that called attention to it as not only a word, but a mark, . . . the visible trace of a touch, a sign that someone had palpably dwelt, however momentarily, on the surface of an artifact," rightly reflects Churchill's sentiments here.[15] He rejects and refuses not simply the work of authorship but the very stuff of authorship—"letters," "spelling," and "writing," which become the detritus of fate's "spite"—as well as a specifically author-centered vision in which the author's "markedness" is the only legitimate form of authorship remaining, since even the developmental stages of the author's craft, namely reading and writing, are evacuated of concrete meaning:

> Much are the precious hours of youth misspent,
> In climbing Learning's rugged steep ascent;
> When to the top the bold advent'rer's got,
> He reigns, vain monarch, o'er a barren spot,
> Whilst in the *vale of Ignorance* below,
> FOLLY and VICE to rank luxuriance grow;
> Honours and wealth pour in on ev'ry side,
> And proud Preferment rolls her golden tide. (5–12)

The utter uselessness of learning ironically generates its own "sterility" as the poet, the unique cipher for authorship in the poem, "reigns . . . o'er a barren spot." From those empty heights, the valley of ignorance energizes and enervates authorship in contradictory images of luxuriance and fluid movement that move not necessarily in the opposite direction (down) from the poet's misspent ascent but rather down and out. Additionally, the nature of the "rolling" golden tide suggests such movement is not only unilateral but bidirectional, and thus "mechanical" movement that culminates in Churchill's most invective word in the poem: "preferment." Preferment here is political strategy as well as concession, and in the toxic, nihilistic environment of authorship, the ideal condition under which such rolling flourishes.

Such flourishing yokes authorship and writing in necessarily bureaucratic ways:

> But *Now*, when DULLNESS rears aloft her throne,
> When LORDLY vassals her wide Empire own,
> When Wit, seduced by *Envy*, starts aside,
> And basely leagues with Ignorance and Pride,
> What *Now* should tempt us, by false hopes misled,
> Learning's unfashionable paths to tread;
> To bear those labours, which our Fathers bore,
> That Crown with-held, which They in triumph wore? (31–38)

Taking his cue from Pope's *Dunciad*, Churchill sketches a bleak vision of Dullness's empire, which she rules through the delegation of her "lordly vassals." Ancient wit, here seduced by "envy," permits modern political values to encroach upon its purity. To the extent that it is substituted with the now institutionally defined and politically rewarded, "learning" is no longer an ascent but merely a "path." The italicized emphasis on "now" indicates that contemporary culture has flattened the way to learning and consequently replaced true authorities with mere "vassals." That is precisely why Churchill ends the stanza with a specifically patrilineal deployment of his thematic sterility. Sons now labour as did their fathers, but sons now do not reap the same rewards. As learning has replaced wit, and vassals authors, so too has the patrilineal guarantee of success been replaced by intellectual sycophancy that serves and is served by preferment alone.

That rot at the heart of institutional structures of empire, and the literature and learning they produce, spreads virus-like to authorial relations between literary tradition and patron. As political structures fail, so too do literary structures of authority. Churchill, though, renders these failures in a specifically geographic instantiation of empire: the land. In a series of proclamations, he sketches the broken, shattered land that once was great:

> Is this the Land,
> Where, Merit and Reward went hand in hand,
> where Heroes, Parent-like, the Poet view'd?
> . . . .
>
> Is this the Land, where on our SPENCER's tongue,
> Enamour'd of his voice, Description hung?
> . . . .
>
> Is this the Land, where, mindful of her charge
> And Office high, fair Freedom walk'd at large;
> Where, finding in our laws a sure defence,
> She mock'd at all restraints, but those of Sense?
> . . . .
>
> Is this the Land, where, in some tyrant's reign,
> When a *weak, wicked Ministerial* train,
> The tools of pow'r, the slaves of int'rest, plann'd
> Their Country's ruin, and with bribes unman'd
> Those wretches, who, ordain'd in Freedom's cause,
> Gave up our liberties, and sold our laws?
> . . . .
>
> Is this the Land, where, in those worst of times,
> The hardy Poet rais'd his honest rimes
> To dread rebuke, and bade controulment speak

In guilty blushes on the villain's cheek,
Bade Pow'r turn pale, kept might rogues in awe,
And made them fear the Muse, who fear'd not the Law?
(51–53, 57–58, 63–66, 73–78, 87–92)

The constellation of rhetorical questions frames the declension of the "land" as a home for virtuous and robust authorship. Starting with the claim that England was once the land where poets were considered "parent-like," and thus a substitute for the kind of sterile *in loco parentis* of bureaucratic authorship earlier in the poem, the interrogative sequence of "is this the land?" reiterates as it describes the continuing downfall of English authorship. From Spencer's descriptions, to the kind of writing that bolsters the law with only "Sense" as its restraint, the lines finally bring affective relief from sorrow. This is indeed a quasi-romantic but ultimately unsustainable mode of poetry for Churchill, since his description soon turns to the weak, wicked ministerial train and their acts that echo the complaints of the *North Briton,* namely the surrendering of liberty for a mere exercise of an unnamed but suggested prerogative.

Indeed, there is another culminating term in this series of questions that serves the same function in this poem as prerogative does in the *North Briton,* namely "controulment." Such "controulment" is a species of preferment, as Churchill makes clear some twenty lines later:

All sacred is the name and pow'r of Kings,
All States and Statesmen are those mighty Things
Which, howsoe'er they out of course may roll,
Were never made for Poets to control. (123–26)

Of course, it does not ultimately matter how those statesmen "roll" off course, because preferment's "tide," as Churchill had proclaimed in his second stanza, performs the "golden roll," and "out" here in the poem is equally an indication of the bidirectional, self-contained nature of preferment. That surely is what poets were never meant to control because from the start it destabilized their once learned positions in the "land," which Churchill is careful to designate with the more precise "country" (139) later in the poem. If preferment grants authors power and authority in Churchill's contemporary world, then "controulment" is the deliberately obsolete term Churchill uses to frame and amplify the ironic distance between contemporary England and the land it once was, that which poets once had but exactly what they lost when preferment became the politically motivated mechanism for authorial definition and success.[16] Such a loss highlights in relief a wilful forgetting of the responsibilities of power and the pervasive politicization of poetry as a form of power in which minsters and poets are interchangeable and in which real poets, with "honest rimes," are forced into supporting freedom as much by criticizing ministers as by raising "parent-like" heroes.

Faced with such a desperate reality, Churchill, having anticipated the sentiment with "controulment," asks the question Paine would find so compelling in *Crisis II:* "What's in this name of Lord that we should fear / To bring their vices to the public ear?" (157–58). The question is the natural corollary of poetry's lost ability and moral responsibility to "speak controulment." Lance Bertelsen notes: "For Churchill there are no valid universal or homogenous rules of behaviour. He advocates a doctrine of individual conscience and judgement, rejecting traditional wisdom for a more spontaneous response based on context and intuition—an ethical stance that bears both an analogous and affective relationship to the structure of his poetry." The very structural function of the question, here repeated, suggests that the lack of an answer is its own kind of answer to the question.[17] Poets ought not fear the mere name of "Lord," and should bring their vices to a public that will reinvigorate the role of the poet and poetry in Churchill's contemporary culture, but they hesitate; they fail to consider either "context" or "intuition" on account of preferment's rolling tide. Preferment elides context and intuition into place and institution. This is the very "disintegration of the disliked" that Morris Golden has noted in Churchill's poetry, and redirected and redounded as it is in these lines back towards the poet as much as the "lords," such disintegrative impulses validate authorship only in relation to its ability to speak about such political realities.

That is the problem of the author. As much as those traditional models are appealing and imbued with a moral authority that was at once critical and yet affective, it is the need for spontaneity as a viable alternative that even preferment removes. What emerges for Churchill is a self-contradictory author of the new regime who, "To virtue lost, to Vice alone . . . wakes, / Most lusciously declaims 'gainst luscious themes, / And, whilst he rails at blasphemy, blasphemes" (388–90). This is truly the authorship of the times, characterized as that of "reflexivity and contradiction," which were "actual modes of perception and action."[18] Indeed true, but the conditions under which those "modes of thought and action" emerge and the arts authors have to conjure in order to succeed in those modes force Churchill to his final stanza and question:

Are these the Arts, which Policy supplies?
Are these the steps, by which grave Churchmen rise?
Forbid it, Heav'n; or should it turn out so,
Let Me, and Mine, continue mean and low.
Such be their Arts, whom Interest controls;
KIDGELL and *I* have free and honest souls.
We scorn Preferment which is gain'd by Sin,
And will, tho' poor without, have peace within. (391–98)

The stanza is a virtuoso performance that draws upon the poem's earlier themes to propel Churchill into a "peace within" that is tenuous and fundamentally unstable. Policy has become a Muse, and inspiration is reduced to mere supply. In his most artful line, Churchill evokes his initial ascent to learning, which was there rendered useless; here it is specifically divided, broken, and ordered into "steps," and by those steps "grave," and therefore "serious" churchmen "rise" in stature and preferment, with the rhyme between "supplies" and "rise" reinforcing that reading. And yet "grave" is also the place of death, a falling and not a rising, unless, of course, one such as a churchman believes in the Resurrection, in which case the grave is a place from which one will rise, but this is a poem where "Christ is laid neglected on a shelf / And the vile priest is Gospel to himself" (381–82).

More so than a critique of Church preferment, Churchill is offering images of the man who turns against himself, the priest who is his own gospel, who lusciously declaims against luscious themes and blasphemes as he rails against blasphemy, "the object given an exaggerated neutrality which can alternatively be expressed as an uncertainty as to its identity."[19] Such uncertainty is the useful contradiction, the thing against which his own final claim is tested. Churchill emerges as the author who "scorns preferment" and thus all the social acceptance and cultural authority that it will bring, and instead "will, tho poor without, have peace within," a contradiction that nonetheless suggests a coherent and complete sense of an authorial self. And nothing reinforces that sense of selfhood, tied to authorship, so much as the release and return of "control." That once power of the author, so central to Churchill, is here given over to "Interest," handmaiden of preferment and the prior condition of preferment as a political policy. With that given over, and his own remaining mean and low, it is not simply that Churchill dwells in his own valley, though not of ignorance. It is that, having come to terms with the new conditions of authorship and definitions of the author, Churchill is, if not content, then certain that what he gets is a self-reflective selfhood from which such "peace" emerges, as much contested as contented.

This poetic mixture of ministerial criticism, authorial lament, and a contest of personalities helps Paine frame much of his second *Crisis* paper. It was published in direct response to the British Proclamation of Conciliation, published on November 30, 1776, and authored by the Howe brothers. William Howe had specifically been commissioned to sue for peace, or at least favorable terms of American surrender, and their proclamation—which commanded that "in order to the more effectual Accomplishment of His Majesty's most gracious intentions, and the speedy Restoration of the public Tranquillity, . . . We Do, in His Majesty's name, and by Virtue of the Powers committed to Us, hereby charge and command all Persons whosoever, who are assembled together in arms against his Majesty's Government, to disband"—was the last of a series that had been published throughout 1776.[20] The proclamation was addressed primarily to colonial families in New Jersey, promising them full pardons, the return of property, and a peace enforced by the British. Paine takes all of that into consideration as he casts the war as one not simply of print culture but of the authorial personalities borne of that culture: "Your lordship, I find, has now commenced author, and published a proclamation; I have published a *Crisis*. As they stand, they are the antipodes of each other; both cannot rise at once, and one of them must descend; and so quick is the revolution of things, that your lordship's performance, I see, has already fallen many degrees from its first place, and is now just visible on the edge of the political horizon."[21] Paine's typical rhetorical sharpness is used to great effect here. Howe's proclamation, an official document of the British government but one that holds no force of law in America, is already losing whatever putative political power it has because speedy revolutions render such proclamations meaningless and thus of merely liminal value on the "edge" of the "political horizon." Given Paine's attendance at James Ferguson's astronomy lectures in the 1750s, it bears noting that for Ferguson, the horizon was that which "limit[s] our view all around."[22] "Just visible" on the political horizon, Howe is he whose very existence and proclamations limit the views of Paine's readers.

This teetering of Howe's proclamation is a reflection of Paine's most Churchillian of understandings concerning the coexistence of these two forms of literary discourse, which may exist in the same plane but cannot occupy the same space, as they form mutually exclusive "antipodes." Paine's geographic metaphor is defined as "places on the earth directly opposite to each other," and such opposition means simply that these two forms of political writing, one a proclamation, the other a crisis, cannot stand conterminous nor occupy even a contested political space with each other. It is, then, a form both of the Churchillian "neutrality" that questions the other object's identity and also of his "terms of nullity—sterility, uselessness, disintegration, invisibility, ambiguity, finally nothingness."[23] Together, the neutrality of Howe's proclamation as the ultimate limiting entity, evacuated of its meaning and intention, along with the geographic and geospatial nullity of the proclamation in relation specifically to Paine's own *Crisis*, posits the contention of that very *Crisis* to be both personal and literary, a contest of conflicted identities between Paine and Howe as much as between his proclamation and Paine's *Crisis*.

This identity dimension becomes evident in the subsequent paragraph, as Paine couches his description in familiar poetic terms: "It is surprising to what a pitch of infatuation, blind folly and obstinacy will carry mankind, and your lordship's drowsy proclamation is a proof that it does not even quit them in their sleep. Perhaps you thought America too was taking a nap, and therefore chose, like Satan to Eve, to whisper delusion softly, lest you should awaken her."[24] Alluding to book 5 of *Paradise Lost*, the passage moves Howe from a Churchillian state of neutrality to a Miltonic state of evil incarnate. In recounting her dream to Adam, Milton's Eve recalls:

> I rose as at thy call, but found thee not;
> To find thee I directed then my walk;
> And on, methought, alone I pass'd through ways
> That brought me on a sudden to the Tree
> Of interdicted Knowledge. (48–52)

Howe's proclamation offers to America that same kind of "interdicted knowledge" in its cozening lies and promises of protection. Howe himself also makes the same mistake that Satan does in book 5: he confuses his own inclination to sleep, and unconsciousness, with America's. It is specifically that blurring of identities, or failure to account for differences in identity and "pitch," that makes Howe out to be nothing short of the devil, since it is that which forms the core of Satan's temptation of Eve in *Paradise Lost:*

> Happie though thou art;
> Happier thou mayst be, worthier canst not be:
> Taste this, and be henceforth among the Gods
> Thy self a Goddess, not to Earth confind,
> But somtimes in the Air, as wee, sometimes

Ascend to Heav'n, by merit thine, and see
What life the Gods live there, and such live thou. (75–81)[25]

Vicki Vickers has noted Paine's indebtedness to Milton in *Common Sense:* "In choosing Satan's word and actions as illustration for his arguments he became—quite literally—the Devil's Advocate."[26] I would suggest that in *Crisis II* Paine progresses in his adaption of *Paradise Lost.* No longer a "devil's advocate," Paine here is a kind of Adam, warning America-as-Eve of the "drowsy" whisper of Satan hoping to give her not independence but knowledge that would save her.

Of course, as one rises between Paine and Howe, so one descends, and the reference to book 5 suggests not only the temptation of Eve but Adam's role and Eve's utter dependence on him, since Eve says of him, "O Sole in whom my thoughts find all repose, / My Glorie, My Perfection" (28–29), and he of Eve, "Best Image of my self and dearer half" (95). This reciprocal identity in book 5 is deconstructed by Satan's attempted dream seduction of Eve; they are the same but there is an underlying and yet to be realized, although already exploited, difference between Adam and Eve. That for Paine in *Crisis II* is a difference with a crucial distinction, as it places Paine and Howe on their respective antipodes. If Howe's own proclamation, promising a kind of forbidden knowledge, rests on his taking for granted the differences between himself and the people to whom he proclaims, then Paine references *Paradise Lost* to show how he as Adam and America as Eve acknowledge a difference that makes all of the difference. It is, after all, Adam who "whispers" Eve awake (17) and Satan who "Close at [her] ear . . . call'd . . . With gentle voice" (36–37).

It is in this Miltonic matrix of adamic salvation and satanic temptation that Paine again borrows from Churchill's poetic repertoire to counter Howe's proclamatory seductions. Not only has Howe confused his own drowsiness for America's, he has also failed to account for the reason why America never sleeps: "This continent, sir, is too extensive to sleep all at once, and too watchful, even in its slumbers, not to startle at the unhallowed foot of an invader."[27] Paine invokes another familiar trope from *Common Sense,* namely "the continent," and here it is America's broad expanse and sheer size that would prevent Howe's proclamation from having any real effect. In referencing specific New Jersey towns such as Burlington, Bordentown, Trenton, Mount Holly, and Princeton, Paine's point is at once tactical and poetic. Howe's proclamation was targeted to the Jersey towns through which the British army was marching, and Paine makes clear that as the army advanced, its inability to hold a location securely with lines so wide-spread meant there could be no meaningful enforcement of the terms of the proclamation. Paine always expresses this in terms of the ever-shrinking circle, poised in opposition to America's and his own *Crisis* paper's extent: "We dishonour ourselves by attacking such trifling characters while greater ones are suffered to escape; 'tis our duty to find *them* out, and their proper punishment would be to exile them from the continent for ever. The circle of them is not so great as some imagine."[28] To exile them from the continent would be to disconnect "such trifling characters" from the kind of "mythic power" the continent as a concept held for Paine, and the ever-shrinking circle, like the edge of the political horizon, is a place that soon reflects a deeply Churchillian sensibility of nullity where such nullity is equated with the geographic specificity of the Jerseys: "Your authority in the Jerseys is now reduced to the small circle which your army occupies; and your procla-mation is no where seen unless it be to be laughed at. The mighty subduers of the continent have retreated into a nutshell."[29] The space of Howe's proc-lamation is reduced from circle to nutshell, from occupying space to a fine point of near negative infinity.

That kind of "retreat" defines Howe's own tactical failures: "I laugh at your notion of conquering America. Because you lived in a little country, where an army might run over the whole in a few days, and where a single company of soldiers might put a multitude to a rout, you expected to find it the same here. It is plain that you brought over with you all the narrow notions you were bred up with."[30] "Little" and "narrow" hem Howe to an inverse infinitude, predicated on the very Miltonic theme from earlier in the paper: his inability to distinguish himself from his object, since he "expected it to be the same here." This is a very Churchillian viewpoint, since Chur-chill often dealt with "the mind's ability to grasp its objects and to make a coherent world of the things which it grasps," and Howe as imagined in *Crisis II* is a man, general, and seducer who fails to intuit the distinction between the mind that grasps and the objects thus grasped, often hampered by expectation.[31] I would like to suggest, however, that just as the increasing smallness of Howe as the *Crisis* paper continues is a function of Paine's Churchillian influence, so too is the contrast of the continent leveraged to diminish Howe. This is the very "politics of size" that was part of Paine's "need to produce a new way of thinking about the extended colonies that would neutralize the deeply appealing but divisive rhetoric of local attach-ment while offering a convincing model of the continent as an autonomous unit rather than a series of disintegrating colonial fragments."[32] Having cohered that neutralization around independence and the success of *Common Sense,* Paine moves on to its corollary as expressed in *Crisis II,* namely the attack on Howe for attempting to exploit the no longer valid "disintegrating colonial fragments." Paine invokes through the use of the continent the very same ideals as Churchill did in the "Is this the Land" section of "The Author." If there his evocation of an equally mythic land, no less than Paine's continent, had meant to cohere disparate strains of authorship, only to conclude with criticism of the "weak, wicked ministerial train," then here is the essential act necessary to both the author's function and that train's success: control.

Control is nowhere to be found in *Crisis II,* but Paine's version of it is invoked in deliberate relation to the continental and ever-shrinking status of Howe and his army, specifically through the use of the word "command." Paine writes of Howe, "Your master has commanded, and you have not enough of nature left to refuse."[33] Coming as the culmination of his paragraph on Howe as Satan, Paine's insult looks both ahead and behind in his *Crisis* paper. It looks behind in the sense that part of Paine's universal empire was not to "command" but to assign—to recommend and outline, not to tell on authority. Paine inverts the circumstances of command here, suggesting that Howe has been commanded, and that his failure is the inability to say no to such a command. In other words, to both lack control and be unable to defy control when it is exerted upon him. This further separates Paine and Howe as it introduces one of Paine's most important themes and images in the *Crisis* paper: nature. Esoterically defined, Paine invests nature with a palpable notion of both moral propriety and deliberate disobedience.[34] Howe's nature is a lack, a negative space that his master fills with his "command." Howe is powerless to resist but also lacks the basic human nature to rebel and revolt against an authority whose control over him is absolute but also absolutely to be resisted.[35]

Paine will twice more use Howe's "nature" to play against his military failures, and each instance has its own deliberate Churchillian connection. The next occurs within a passage in which Paine indicates the shrinking circle of Howe's Jersey army and expedition, and when speaking of men's characters, claims: "Some men have naturally a military turn, and can brave hardships and the risk of life with a cheerful face; others have not; no slavery appears to them so great as the fatigue of arms, and no terror so powerful as that of personal danger. What can we say? We cannot alter nature, neither ought we to punish the son because the father begot him in a cowardly mood."[36] Paine's first claim reifies his earlier ones on Howe's subservient and servile nature; it reinforces the limits and extent of control that Howe only begins to think he exercises. Such inalterability is not a fault, however, for as much as Paine discusses the variety of men's characters when it comes to the "fatigue of arms," it is for a Churchillian climax that Paine suggests that the sons cannot be blamed for their cowardly begetting. Just as Churchill had focused on the "parent-like" poet and the disintegrative properties of patrilineal heredity as signs of poetic merit and authorship in his contemporary culture, so too does Paine suggest that while the power of patrilineal heredity remains, its effects and consequences vitiate power such that the nature of the result is unalterable but nonetheless highly regrettable, and ultimately cowardly if not completely dissociative. Such power falsely engenders the belief, held by Howe, in its own similitude to its objects of knowledge.

Leveraged in *Crisis II* as a Churchillian weapon against Howe, the evocation of nature results in one of Paine's most famous lines: "This is my creed of politics. If I have any where expressed myself over-warmly, 'tis from a fixed, immovable hatred I have, and ever had, to cruel men and cruel measures. I have likewise an aversion to monarchy, as being too debasing to the dignity of man; but I never troubled others with my notions till very lately, nor ever published a syllable in England in my life. What I write is pure nature, and my pen and my soul have ever gone together."[37] In one short sentence, Paine rejects any notion of a radical print ideology that reduces the role of authorial personality. Indeed, Paine has allowed his definition of authorship to "be put to use: as a shorthand for the value (or lack thereof) of a given text or reader or writer, or a set of tacit instructions as to what should be done with that text, or reader, or writer, . . . or a sign of where that text or reader or writer should be located—literarily, socially, geographically."[38] To state his creed in politics is for Paine to do no less than Churchill did at the end of "The Author," namely to assert the essential framework of his own identity and the suite of practices and dispositions that constitute that identity. For Churchill, it was a viable, functional disparity between external poverty and internal peace, the opposite and the living challenge to the solipsistically self-reflexive, self-absorbed poets of his age. For Paine, his "creed" harkens back to his role as authentic "defender of the faith" and guarantor of reasonable rebellion, but that creed in politics is only assured, and truly believed in, because of Paine's own self-description, his own self-reflexive emphasis on "pen and soul" going together and his writing of nature. If Churchill's point was the intra-fluid dimensions of the modern author, of which Howe's shrinking is a form and species, then Paine here resists fluidity, and contends against it by suggesting that his "pen" (external) and "soul" (internal) are a unity—distinct, individuated things that go together like Churchill's peace and poverty. Indeed to some extent it is Paine's "peace" here.[39] As well, the writing of nature on the surface is the writing of what nature demands or what Howe's nature lacks: the will to subordinate commands and reject what Paine claims is his deepest aversion. Such nature constitutes the very control that Churchill lacked, as well as the scope of prerogative with which Paine had opened the paper, and as such, Paine creates, no less than Churchill, an evocative, coherent authorial self, able to insist upon and justify his final claim: "A lasting independent peace is my wish, end and aim; and to accomplish that, *I pray God the Americans may never be defeated, and I trust while they have good officers, and are well commanded,* and willing to be commanded, *that they* NEVER WILL BE."[40]

Paine brings his *Crisis* paper full circle. He has bequeathed his own authorial recognition that he "cannot command obedience" and responsibility to "assign duty." Both are revolutionary dictates of the author, tied to the martial activities of not simply the revolutionary army but of Americans as a whole. In so doing, Paine creates what Nancy Ruttenberg has called a "democratic personality," which "far from representing a conscientious or reasoned anticipation of such [liberal-democratic] values, . . . adumbrate[s] the untheorized, experiential beginnings of political life for a person without a public voice within the culture."[41] For Paine, that democratic personality emerges out of the echoes of his own authorial description in the opening paragraph to the emergence of "untheorized" Americans in this his last, coalesced around the word "command," both echo and prolepsis. Command, of course, harkens back to the universal empire of the writer's prerogative, but it also demonstrates that for Paine and the project of American liberty, the command of informed obedience is the genuine assignation of duty: Americans can accept the latter because of how they perform and embody the former. They are not so much coterminous as existing, in Paine's own vocabulary, as cispodean entities, with the Americans able to be both "well commanded" and "willing" to be commanded. Assuredly those same Americans have enough of nature, perhaps even Paine's own, to understand the commands, but the phrasing here is of particular importance. The virtue of command runs both ways; it is both an attribute of the American officers and likewise a quality and function of the Americans themselves. Their will to be commanded does not merely compliment their officers' command, it fulfils and establishes the grounds of the very independence that Paine so strenuously supports. In Churchillian terms, they have come to difficult terms with the spectre of Howe and his tendency to redound the nature of his arguments within himself; they have transcended the simple binary that both Churchill and Paine establish in their works and stand as the unified, coherent body that both claims as right and fights for as prize the independence Howe would have them forsake. This then is the "controulment" Churchill found so necessary and yet so elusive. If in "The Author" he could only lament its loss and ascribe it to the hands of "Interest," then Paine does him one better and puts it to the service of independence.

FIVE

The Field of Imagination

Public and Private Spheres in Paine's Manuscript Poetry

The natural bent of my mind was to science. I had some turn, and I believe some talent, for poetry; but this I rather repressed than encouraged, as leading too much into the field of imagination.

—*The Age of Reason*, part 1, chapter 7

Thomas Paine dismisses nearly three decades worth of his poetical writing with a single sentence buried in an early section of his deist masterpiece, *The Age of Reason*. Commenting on orthodox Christianity's "corruption" of science and his own contemporary appeal to science as the most genuine theological system, Paine rejects and "represses" not just his own native talent for poetry but poetry itself as a literary genre too inclined to imagination. In all, it is a public declamation of the epistemological ends of print culture, in as much as the fixity and standardization of print had for Paine achieved a kind of "natural" scientific fixity in which poetry had no place as a way of knowing. As such practices spread, poetry diminishes in inverse ratio, a figment of imagination and not a product of science. And yet, contemporaneously with these claims for the dominance of print logic on the fields of knowledge, Paine would write some of his most intensely passionate, lyrical, and imaginative poetry in manuscript. Publicly rejecting but privately writing poetry, Paine is making no less than a claim for poetry within the public and private spheres. As a genre with both public connotations and private functions, poetry articulates not so much the constituent differences between those two spheres but their boundary, that against which Paine measures the public sphere's rejection of imagination as reasonable discourse and the private sphere's embrace of affective reality as a viable, alternative means not merely of knowing but of determining what exactly ought to be known.

Perhaps surprisingly, Paine discusses poetry at length in *The Age of Reason,* primarily in the context of biblical writers identified as prophets and the generic construction of their eponymous Old Testament books. Rapidly coursing through other biblical books, Paine in chapter 7 of part 1 soon lights upon the prophets: "All the remaining parts of the Bible, generally known by the name of the Prophets, are the works of the Jewish poets and itinerant preachers, who mixed poetry, anecdote, and devotion together—and those works still retain the air and style of poetry, though in translation."[1] Paine's essential argument is based on linguistic change; the prophets are merely poets who later came to be considered prophets-as-seers. They have no inherent ability to see the future, much less predict it correctly, and only historical anachronism mistakes mere poetry for prophecy and future-seeing.[2] The reason for the shift, according to Paine, is not simply one historical change or Christian (and latently Jewish) wish fulfillment and mythmaking. Instead, it lies in the nature of poetry itself, which he explains in a long footnote:

> Poetry consists principally in two things—imagery and composition. The composition of poetry differs from that of prose in the manner of mixing long and short syllables together. Take a long syllable out of a line of poetry, and put a short one in the room of it, or put a long syllable where a short one should be, and that line will lose its poetical harmony. It will have an effect upon the line like that of misplacing a note in a song. The imagery in these books, called the Prophets, appertains altogether to poetry. It is fictitious, and often extravagant, and not admissible in any other kind of writing than poetry.[3]

Paine's double definition of poetry as complementary imagery and composition, such that certain images can only belong to poetic composition ("not admissible in any other kind of writing"), anticipates his later rejection of it. The description of the structural composition of poetry is simple enough. The meter of the line demands certain words that match meter, and a simple switch-out for an unmetrical word in the line disorders the whole, rendering it, in Paine's term, "unharmonious." And yet despite the inherent symmetry and natural cohesion of imagery and composition, its very "appertainability," it is the substance of imagery that is deeply problematic. At once "fictitious" and "extravagant," biblical poetry has the specific problem of saying nothing substantial about God, His "system," or even the depth of feeling with which the prophet prophecies. Indeed, poetry's problem, as reflected in the linguistic frame with which Paine opens, is that it often, if not always, confuses those three things for the same thing.

Paine highlights this with a sample of on-the-spot poetry:

> To show that these writings are composed in poetical numbers, I will take ten syllables, as they stand in the book, and make a line of the same number of syllables, (heroic measure) that shall rhyme with the last word. It will then be seen that the composition of these books is poetical measure. The instance I shall produce is from Isaiah:
>
> *"Hear, O ye heavens, and give ear, O earth!"*
> 'Tis God himself that calls attention forth.
>
> Another instance I shall quote is from the mournful Jeremiah, to which I shall add two other lines, for the purpose of carrying out the figure, and showing the intention of the poet:
>
> *"O! that mine head were waters and mine eyes"*
> Were fountains flowing like the liquid skies;
> Then would I give the mighty flood release,
> And weep a deluge for the human race.[4]

Taking Isaiah 1:2 and Jeremiah 9:1 from the King James Bible, Paine shows how easily the prophets can be rendered poetic, but also how, practically enslaved to the meter of the lines, the imagery can be fabricated from nothing and only because the metrical structure of the line allows that kind of imagery. The original verses in the King James Bible read, "Hear, O heavens, and give ear, O earth: for the LORD hath spoken, I have nourished and brought up children, and they have rebelled against me" (Isaiah 1:2), and "Oh that my head were waters, and mine eyes a fountain of tears, that I might weep day and night for the slain of the daughter of my people!" (Jeremiah 9:1). Neither of Paine's lines perfectly replicate those verses, but his claim that the figure in Jeremiah carries itself "out" in his own rendering of the lines demonstrates, with evidence, that the poets can make up their imagery as substitutes for what they purportedly really wish to say. Poetry then is the kind of writing that can only be poetry, and whose language so closely adheres to the generic conventions of poetry that it cannot be anything other than what it is. This is why the mere biblical word for poet (prophet) later came to mean someone who sees into the future or seems to predict future events: the register of poetry as esoteric imagery tied inexorably to rigid metrical patterns gives the appearance of proleptic persuasion, knowledge of the future, and grasp of moral ills. If one is able to simply make up the imagery, it is equally easy to make up the consequences and importance of that imagery to belief, and to substitute one's own narratives for objective knowledge, or perhaps most importantly, attempts at constructing objective knowledge. This is for Paine above all an aberrant and spurious form of knowledge, and the utter ease with which he casually renders the biblical prophets into poetry (even in translation) practically unfolds such aberrance before his readers' very eyes, itself a form of knowledge obviously more scientific than the prophet-poets'. Poetry inevitably speaks only about itself.

Having dispensed with poetry as prophecy, Paine states his major case for deism: that the knowable universe, observable by science alone, is the perfect theology. And while Paine will claim that prophecy was a term of science "promiscuously applied" to poetry, his discussion of the orthodox Christian suppression of scientific knowledge slips necessarily into autobiography and a calculated reference to poetry: "The natural bent of my mind was to science. I had some turn, and I believe some talent, for poetry; but this I rather repressed than encouraged, as leading too much into the field of imagination."[5] Paine had treated imagination both before and after the publication of *The Age of Reason*, in *A Letter Addressed to the Abbé Raynal* (1782) and *An Essay on Dream* (1800), but his claim for poetry leading him too much into the field of imagination marks the first and only time he ties that intellectual faculty in which he took an occasional interest with a specific literary genre, a genre which had, as I have tried to argue, played a vital role in his literary and political writings up to this time. Imagination, especially as it functioned in the 1790s, has been described by John Whale as "an integral figure in cultural critique and . . . a complex, often creative, response to cultural change."[6] For Paine, its function as a cultural critique of Christianity necessitated an outright rejection of imagination's bent toward creativity as potentially damaging to the larger political and epistemological needs of that culture.

In *A Letter Addressed to the Abbé Raynal*, Paine offers a relatively positive vision of imagination, listing it with "passion and judgement" as the "three powers of the mind" and noting that "a certain degree of animation must be felt by the writer, and raised in the reader, in order to interest the attention; and a sufficient scope given to the imagination, to enable it to create in the mind a sight of the persons, characters and circumstances of the subject: for without these, the judgment will feel little or no excitement to office, and its determinations will be cold, sluggish, and imperfect."[7] Here, imagination catalyses a reader's engagement with a text and the subsequent making of meaning, which in turn makes imagination the constituent spur to its sister faculty judgment. While Paine immediately goes on to caution that "if either of the two former (imagination and passion) are raised too high, or heated too much, the judgment will be jostled . . . and the whole matter will diminish into a pantomime of the mind," it is nonetheless the case that despite its potential to enthusiastically jostle judgment, imagination is the premier intellectual faculty that both permits and creates Paine's claim later in the *Letter* that "repeated experience has shown, not only the impracticality of conquering America, but the still higher impossibility of conquering her mind, or recalling her back to her former condition of thinking."[8] It is ultimately imagination that both pushes Americans past that brink and, valve-like, prevents them from going back.

Some twenty years later, in 1800, when Paine published *An Essay on Dream*, his assessment of imagination's role in the intellectual faculties and political history had deteriorated. Paine forgoes passion as a power of the mind, replacing it with the rather more conventional memory. While he acknowledges that the operations of memory, imagination, and judgment have some resemblance to a "watch," he gives imagination the role of "the main spring which puts all in motion," yet also calls it the most "volatile" of the three faculties.[9] Imagination renders dreams "a riotous assemblage of misshapen images and ranting ideas," ascribing the eighteenth century's most notorious image of social disorder to imagination's proclivities. Most tellingly and thus damningly, imagination ultimately "cannot supply the place of real memory, it has the wild faculty of counterfeiting memory."[10] In parallel, imagination creates "counterfeit realities," but more disruptively it "has no idea of time," substituting infinite progression for rational relation, and mimics memory such that when things are forgotten and imaginatively, not genuinely, remembered, "it is ourselves asking ourselves the question."[11]

The essentially solipsistic questioning of imagination in *An Essay on Dream* is a closed loop similar to how poetry works for Paine in *The Age of Reason*. Whale contends that for Paine, "imagination, as a sign of an erroneous and divisive political system, must be exposed as false and absurd," consequently rendering Paine an "iconoclast." But I would contend that, as demonstrated in his claims about poetry in *The Age of Reason*, Paine still acknowledges yet is wary of the deep intellectual and political power of imagination, specifically because it is so inherently attached to a literary genre like poetry.[12] Indeed, Paine's statement in *The Age of Reason* about his own inclination to poetry centers around a related constellation of terms: "bent," "turn," "talent," and "repress." Paine's tendency to equate individualism to geometry has been noted and here that equation becomes central to his rejection of poetry.[13] He begins by claiming that his "natural bent" is toward science, suggesting not simply an individual proclivity but a special geometrical relationship within the "bending degree of curvature."[14] While not a straight line, such curvature is "natural" to the shape of the mathematical construction of curves, and it offers an image of Paine in close geometrical proximity to the sciences; his own inclination is but one point on the curve proximate to any other point on the curve of the sciences. Of course, the determination of the place and the distance between two points on a curve is a function of calculus, so that Paine's simple, personal statement about his own inclination also describes a relationship determined by the very sciences to which he is inclined.[15]

While Paine's "bent" is toward science, his "turn" and "talent" is for poetry. Paine qualifies both terms with "some," linking them alliteratively and imaginatively as paltry half-measures of poetic ability. "Turn," of course, is a near synonym for "bent," but here, evacuated of its scientific and calculating function, "turn" is essentially a poetical term that indicates a constant rotation, a tendency to rotate on a fixed point infinitely and opposed to the calculable fixed distance between points on a bent curve.[16] That turn, like his talent, is unstable and fundamentally unreliable, and is made so by Paine's deliberately biblical pun on talents. There is a twinkle of Paine's poetic talent at work here, since his language inverts expectation in order to force the point. His bent, as an essentially mathematical function, is "natural," yet the talent, drawn referentially from the Gospel of Matthew (25:14–30) is equally so: a naturally inherited, divinely proffered capacity for something, and something given away at great expense. This then becomes the subject of Paine's "belief," the very act and content of which he spends the entirety of *The Age of Reason* seeking to dismantle and recalibrate to the natural bent of the sciences.

The rejection of poetry thus becomes a microcosm of Paine's entire argument in *The Age of Reason*. By refusing poetry any legitimate role in theological or scientific and thus rational discourse, Paine is simultaneously denying it as a legitimate and thus authoritative literary genre. Yet to do so simultaneously offers poetry as so vital to the constituent intellectual faculty of imagination that it, by necessity as much as compulsion, should be repressed. Repression is the unspoken actor in Paine's other considerations of imagination, the silent intellectual function that regulates the relationship between the faculties and keeps imagination in all cases in check. Here, repression is offered as an intellectual choice that both substitutes for and divides the individual act of will from the divinely appointed talent. This is very much a controlled, "iconoclastic" act of Paine's in relation to his own "talent" and "turn." Repression in this instance is not the antithesis of belief but its eventual, inevitable deconstruction, the intellectual act of individual will that obviates and obliterates the divinely provided, not scientifically functional, gift.

This, then, is how Paine tends his field of imagination. Paine often invoked natural imagery in his political writing, whether it was the tree under which government begins in *Common Sense* or the vegetative end of *The Rights of Man*. That gives his claim here something of a political hue, perhaps even bent, but the "field" is unlike any other description Paine had for imagination. As noted, in *A Letter Addressed to the Abbé Raynal,* imagination is likened to riots and American exceptionalism and thus has both a social and national value. In *An Essay on Dream* imagination is compared to a watch spring and therefore to the mechanical, material world, the dominant metaphor for Paine's own deism. The field appropriately stands somewhere in between these two images. Paine knows enough of James Thomson's work to see that fields have deep social value in the history of English poetry and, while not mechanical, are certainly vibrant examples of the material world as expressed in nature. This to a real extent is what the field is: a limitless, boundless, open expanse; a chasm, gap, and *mise en abyme,* where imagination has no limits to subdue it and can make meaning in total dislocation. Poetry essentially actuates and activates this imaginative potential, and poetry thus becomes the anti-calculus, the literary genre that follows a rigorous, rational rule of meter but puts it to the service of imagery that serves nothing but itself. This is flat, and fields are flat. Perhaps even hilly, but certainly not curved.

Behind this obvious difference, however, lies another hint of Paine's poetic sensitivity. While "bent" typically means "curvature; the space of a curve," it also could mean "a place covered in grass; as opposed to a wood, a bare field, a grassy plain."[17] Paine artfully bookends his disclamation of poetry with two fields. One is "natural" and "bare," enclosed within the image of the curve and knowable, like the universe and God, by the science to which it inclines. The other is the field of imagination: poetic, repressible, and repressed, tending toward enthusiasm and thus beyond any fixed point in reality, embracing and not accommodating the infinite. Paine thus turns away from poetry in *The Age of Reason* as a faulty and essentially dysfunctional literary genre that suits the worst inclinations and habits of a necessary human faculty. Indeed, if Paine admires the systematic nature of the universe as sign of God's presence and science as its essential interpretive tool, then here the field of imagination is deeply, distressingly unsystematic—always leading away, but never toward. Repression is down, the field is out, and, in either direction, poetry is antithetical to the calculable, centripetal curve.

If, though, every act of erasure is a simultaneous act of exposure, then something is bound to be revealed in Paine's attempt to erase poetry from the public record through a private act of repression. Poetry becomes a kind of palimpsest, a genre that only, as Paine suggests, talks to itself and has something to say about itself and not the world as it is. Indeed, it is offered up as a discourse that actively draws the reader away from those realities. Why then did Paine, contemporaneously with these public claims against poetry, write the most intense and passionate lyrical poetry in manuscript? Several scholars have already noted the continued persistence of manuscript poetry in the eighteenth century, and Paine's is no exception.[18] Three manuscript poems are of value in displaying Paine's private attachment to poetry while he was publicly disavowing it. A very different Paine is inscribed in these manuscript poems, closer perhaps to the generally European construct of Paine as a necessarily flexible and meaningfully inconsistent thinker who poses "a problem in knowing how to approach the diverse writings and activities of the writer and polemicist."[19] In terms of Paine's poetry and of the very clear collapse of Paine's belief that poetry could function as an important part of a critical public sphere, this means considering Paine as lyrically sensitive and romantically moody, willing to explore aspects of human experience and ideas that are rich in the very imagination he rejects in *The Age of Reason,* not because those aspects create alternative narratives but because they invest specific narratives with an at once volatile and precious quality that befits their lyrical addressees.[20]

While dates for these manuscript poems can only be approximated, their recipients—Sir Robert Smyth and his wife and the wife of Joel Barlow—suggest that the poems are contemporaneous with *The Age of Reason* and Paine's time in France during and after the French Revolution.[21] "From A Castle in the Air to the Little Corner of the World" is a reference to the epistolary names Paine had shared with the wife of Robert Smyth, a radical financier in France during the revolution.[22] Her chosen name reflects a feminine shyness and proposed modesty standing as bulwark against the global calamity of the revolution, an oasis of feminized calm and peace amidst violence and upheaval. Paine's is a common eighteenth-century poetic and periodical figure used by poets like Christopher Smart in his periodical the *Student* and by Charles Churchill in "The Duellist." Paine opens the poem by describing his own castle in the air:

> In the region of clouds, where the whirlwinds arise,
> My castle of fancy was built;
> The turrets reflected the blue from the skies,
> And the windows with sunbeams were gilt. (1–4)

Paine's castle of fancy, a less refined faculty than imagination, is built in an evocative natural setting of blue skies, golden sunshine, and Zephyr-like whirlwinds, yet the contrasting rhymes of arise/skies and built/gilt reflect the inherent instability and disquiet of the image. While the natural rhymes are in the present tense and infuse the natural imagery with an aura of poetic permanence and presence, the verbs of human work and production, "build" and "guild," are offered in the past tense and suggest the construction of the castle as a work of human agency, tinged with a potentially destructive attachment to the past. Indeed, this aberrant attachment is itself a form of constructed artifice, since "guilding" is merely the layering of gold upon a surface and not an engoldening process.

This initial stanzaic tension between the natural and the constructed, the real and the artificial, is echoed in a familiar Paine poetical device, namely his poetic tendency to render irregular, often professional procedures as striking verbs that propel the action of his poetry:

> The rainbow sometimes, in its beautiful state,
> Enamel'd the mansion around;
> And the figures that fancy in clouds can create,
> Supplied me with garden and ground. (5–8)

Having "built" and "gilt," Paine describes the "beautiful rainbow," swapping blue and gold for a spectrum of color, but such spectral splendor is soon shaped by what it does: "enamel," a word that wraps the castle in a riot of color and likewise suggests a shining, glossy coating that is essentially opaque and not colorful. This is a kind of enforced beauty, as spectral as the clouds that constitute his supply of "garden and ground." The following stanza extends the list of those supplies, as the clouds create "grottoes, and fountains, and orange tree groves" (9). These cirriform natural features lead to a poetic reflection: "I had all that enchantment has told;/I had sweet shady walks, for the Gods and their Loves,/I had mountains of coral and gold" (10–12). Imaginatively evocative but empty of content, the poem itself is structured by, and thereby doomed to, the narrator's attachment to time. All of those enchantments were "had."

The victim of that crushing, perceptible sense of time is the narrator himself, and what results is a loss of feeling:

> But a storm that I felt not, had risen and roll'd,
> While wrapp'd in a slumber I lay;
> And when I look'd out in the morning, behold
> My Castle was carried away. (13–16)

Like "castle in the air," "roll" is a term that Paine borrows from Charles Churchill for maximum effect, and the intensity of the storm's "roll" essentializes the narrator's nonfeeling of it as equally shocking. It is no surprise that "slumber" portends this fanciful flight; Paine's treatment of sleep in *An Essay On Dream* considered it and dreaming as the wilderness of the intellect, which has as much space and capacity for feeling as it does for time. That is why the castle's flight is introduced by the enjambed "behold," lingering at the end of the third line of the stanza like a dangling call to see. That imperative is sharply contrasted by the past tense of "carried away," and, by echoing the first stanza's "My castle of fancy was built," this stanza becomes an emphatic reiteration of the narrator's attachment to the past.

The next stanza plays with this very notion of time, but the intersection of feeling and time modulates the confusing, almost topsy-turvy point of view presented in the poem. The third stanza seems to support a reading of the narrator as watching his castle fly away from him, but the next stanza makes it clear that the castle flies away with him in it. His fanciful journey takes him over "rivers, and valleys, and groves" (17), a natural checklist that provides a new and more holistic viewpoint, since "The world it was all in my view" (18). However, that viewpoint, not so much new as now genuinely visionary and prospective, introduces and triggers thought in the poem: "I thought of my friends, of their fates, of their loves, / And often, full often, of YOU" (19–20). The intra-stanzaic parallels between the rivers, valleys, and groves and the friends, fates, and loves makes them at once symmetrical yet vitally differentiated because the latter set of terms culminates not in a feeling but a person: "you."

This marks a real, seismic shift in the poem at its halfway point. The checklist of rivers, valleys, and groves passed over by the castle of fancy are just more terms of ethereal confabulation, index entries in the catalogue of the narrator's fanciful supplies. The introduction of "thought" exerts radical force in the poem, shifting dread attachment from the past into an iterative present invested in a human person as opposed to failing human agency. This is why nature "makes" in the next stanza a "place . . . but small, but . . . perfectly serene / And checkered with sunshine and shade" (23–24). Balancing shade and light, the "perfect" scene is merely "made," not a product of a verb-rendered human manufacturing process, but in silence by nature as nature. With "sunshine," "shade," "silence," and "beautiful," Paine is deliberately evoking his previous imagery in order for it to be seen—beheld—under the transformative vision of this little corner of the world, and in a sense this is how a castle in the air arrives at a little corner of the world, namely through the seamless transition from ethereal nature and unfeeling fancy to deeply personal affective states:

> I gazed and I envied with painful goodwill,
> And grew tired of my seat in the air;
> When all of a sudden my Castle stood still,
> As if some attraction was there. (25–28)

Calibrating his poetic language to the trajectories of his political writings, Paine ensures that the movement of his affective states, inaugurated by "gazing" through to envy, pain, and fatigue, fashions these newly affective and fully feeling states as the preferred reality to anything described in the poem's first three stanzas because they provide a framework for managing and understanding his fancy *through* feeling. The "as if" is essentially a feint. In a poem that has constructed whole natural settings from clouds and a paradise from fancy, that attraction is the most real object in the poem because it is a force, an elemental reality that exists within and without fancy. That is the strength but also the utter necessity of the simile. Described in the Newtonian language of "attraction," which makes the castle "still," the emergence of these affective states generates a kind of energy that through rest impels the castle of fancy to the little corner, and the narrator to "you."

Susan Stewart has noted, "The history of lyric is . . . the history of a relation between pronouns, the genesis of *ego-tu* and *ego-vos* in the reciprocity of an imagination posing and composing itself and its audience via the work of time."[23] What remains is for the narrator to explore the nature of that work, here read as "attraction":

> Like a lark from the sky it came fluttering down,
> And placed me exactly in view,

When whom should I meet in this charming retreat,
This corner of calmness but YOU.

Delighted to find you in honor and ease,
I felt no more sorrow, nor pain;
But the wind coming fair, I ascended the breeze,
And went back with my Castle again. (29–36)

The delicate "fluttering" strikingly reverses the poem's opening insistence on manufactured verbs and becomes a preamble, the prior, necessary condition of this stanza's reflection of, and improvement upon, the fifth stanza where thought first emerged. This stanza is the direct result of that stanza. If there it was having "the world all in my view," a complete, totalizing vision, that begets thought, then here it is the exactness and idealized calibration ("exactly") of view that allows him to "meet" and opens the space for fancy to become an encounter, a movement from fanciful address to lyrical presence. That presence is summed up in "delight," the first and only genuinely positive feeling and affective state in the poem, at this point a kind of affective correction and comeuppance to the rest of the poem.

I would suggest, however, that a species of lyrical doubt rests in this final stanza, for two related reasons. The first is that given the finding/feeling dynamic in that last stanza, what Paine finds in his delight is not a positive affect but the absence of negative feelings of pain and sorrow. Presence ultimately, perhaps inevitably, causes absence and absence impels return. Harkening back to the opening "whirlwinds," Paine's narrator ascends the breeze and "goes back with the Castle again." This is a return with a difference; rather than returning *to* the castle, as if once again in the first part of the poem, the narrator, emphasized by the iterative and reiterative redundancy of "back" and "again," returns *with* the castle. This is not just a difference; this is all the difference in the world, for it means that by poem's end, in a state of negative delight, the narrator has not just accepted but embraced his affective state, and resigned himself not to repeat his fanciful construction of nature but to transform and translate his act of encounter into an act of accompaniment between his thought and imagination, his feelings and his pains.

Like "Castle in the Air," "Contentment, or If You Please, Confession," a poem Paine wrote to Ruth Barlow, centers around the lyrical exploration of its titular state. It begins,

O could we always live and love,
And always be sincere,

> I would not wish for heaven above,
> My heaven would be here. (1–4)

Using a language of misapprehension about the ability to "always" love and be sincere, Paine offers a secular paradise not in exchange for a divine one but in place of it. His subsequent stanzas go on to describe that earthly paradise:

> Through many countries I have seen,
> And more may chance to see,
> *My Little Corner of the World*
> Is half the world to me;
>
> The other half, as you may guess,
> America contains;
> And thus, between them, I possess
> The whole world for my pains. (5–12)

This is "Castle in the Air" redux; while acknowledging that the sum total of his world is his "little corner of the world" and America, person and nation together, Paine's possession ends in nothing but pain. And, as Stewart has written: "To equate pain with subjectivity is to equate the body with subjectivity and so to confuse the most collective with the most individual. . . . The situation of the person resides in the genesis of the memory of action and experience in intersubjective terms—that is, in the articulation and mastery of the originating pain."[24] In Paine this is the pain of absence, but not one fancied as in "Castle in the Air." Instead, like the distance between heaven and earth, between living and loving and always living and always loving, the distance between Paine and the two halves of his world is an apparently insurmountable gap that can only be automatically filled with the pain both of what he's owed and what he feels, which thus becomes his "whole world."

This near-tragic realization leads to the second half of the poem:

> I'm then contented with my lot,
> I can no happier be;
> For neither world I'm sure has got
> So rich a man as me.
>
> Then send no fiery chariot down
> To take me off from hence,
> But leave me on my heavenly ground—
> This prayer is *common-sense*. (13–20)

If return is the primal urge of "Castle in the Air," here it is to remain, and it is reflection that impels the urge. This reflective turn in the poem, with the "whole world" of pain becoming "contentment with his lot," is finally explained, and indeed so large, steep, and surprising a turn can only be rationalized by a reference to Paine's own work: a common sense that is not so much the foundation of political independence and national sovereignty but the barest of prayerful invocations. It is a prayer not of supplication or thanksgiving but of mere acquiescence and placid resignation in the face of pain. This may seem utterly contrary to what *Common Sense* advocated for America, but the difference is one of degree and not kind, for as Paine ends the poem:

Let others choose another plan,
I mean no fault to find;
The true theology of man
Is *happiness of mind*. (21–24)

Advocating for a poetic right of conscience, Paine acknowledges that his sudden reflective assessment of a "whole world" of pain as a happy and contented lot is troubling, or too easily transformed, and that it should be left to him alone and not as counsel to those who feel the same. This rejection of the universal, moralistic application of Paine's own poetic thinking is the very sum total of "happiness of mind" and mirrors what he says in *The Age of Reason*.[25] Both purport to offer the "true theology of man," and it is here that the import of Paine's title comes to bear. Paine's contentment has been his confession—his admission of pain and, as this final stanza verifies, an admission of guilt in as much as his reflective transformation of total pain into meek acceptance and happiness has no application beyond Paine or his poem. The contentment is the confession, but Paine plays with the notion of confession as both that admission of guilt and a statement of belief. This explains the reference to *Common Sense,* yet it is also the best summation of "happiness of mind," a lyrical version of Paine's "my own mind is my own church."[26] If his mind is his church, then "happiness of mind" is its lyrical creed and confession. His call to let others choose their own plan is not a respectful acknowledgement of others, the purview of the right to choose. It is a provocative challenge for them to actually choose a plan, to embrace contentment as a foundational confession as easily and as individually as he has. "Contentment" ultimately demands to be read as a poetic distillation of *The Age of Reason*.

Dedicated to Sir Robert Smyth, the final poem under consideration, entitled "What is Love?," was written in response to an unpublished letter from Smyth to Paine, which Paine references in a manuscript note atop the American Philosophical Society copy of the poem: "As I do not attempt to rival your witty description of Love I will try if I can match it in sentiments, and that I may start with a fair chance I begin with your own question."[27] That question is the poem's title, and Paine's poetic answer begins,

> 'Tis that delightsome transport we can feel
> Which painters cannot paint, nor words reveal,
> Nor any art we know of can conceal.
>
> Canst thou describe the sunbeams to the blind
> Or make him feel a shadow with his mind?
> So neither can we by description show
> The first of all felicities below. (1–7)

Paine outlines the negative, affective sublime, something not simply felt but felt with "delightsome transport" and which has no correlation in the descriptive realm or through conventional descriptive arts. Indeed, if transportive feeling is what love is, then description is what it eludes, as Paine plays on the paradoxical rhyme of the artist's failure to "reveal" and art's inability to conceal. The contrary expectations of the rhymes are reconciled in their failures to describe that to which they refer. What remains is feeling as the only tangible aspect of the stanza that could be a response, but that too is something other—a transport, and a removal from feeling as much as a feeling itself. This is why the figure and image of the blind man is so compelling. His is a personal, anatomical failure—a personal failure in as much as his own body prevents him from knowing or feeling—and the image suggests that love cannot be described to someone who has not ever or yet felt it.

These are difficult preconditions for answering the question "what is love?," but Paine attempts to do so as the poem continues:

> When happy Love pours magic o'er the soul,
> And all our thoughts in sweet delirium roll;
> When contemplation spreads her rainbow wings,
> And every flutter some new rapture brings;
> How sweetly then our moments glide away,
> And dreams repeat the raptures of the day;

We live in ecstasy, to all things kind,
For love can teach a moral to the mind. (8–15)

The poetic vocabulary is familiarly Paine's ("rainbow," "flutter," "roll")
but the sober, didactic ending seems to derail the language of passion and
intense affect: "delirium," "rapture," "ecstasy," and in this poem "magic,"
which casts the entire stanza in a pixie-dust hue the structure of the stanza
is consistently trying to dispel. Indeed, Paine is never far from seeing love
as an intellectual as much as an affective virtue, and the alternating, nearly
antiphonal nature of the stanza reflects the not-always creative tension between these states. In each set of couplets, the rhyme again works against
the expectation of the lines. Each set contains an image of "thought," each
set contains an image of affective excess. The first three sets of lines are
each joined by the conjunctive "and," which grammatically ties the lines but
essentially unwinds the rhyme connection by establishing the lines as two
distinct sets of ideas, not linked descriptions of love, which Paine has already established as difficult if not impossible to create. The adverbial construction of the first three sets of lines ties them imaginatively together, but
nearly everything in the final couplet wrenches the stanza's meaning away
from a volatile contest between thoughts and affect as the defining conditions of love. The conjunctive "and" becomes the prepositional "for," which
also acts as the declarative statement of a logical conclusion drawn; the adverbial "when" and "how" become the plural pronoun "we." A corresponding universal benevolence is the result, to be and act kindly (though Paine
deliberately elides that distinction) to "all things." That is the moral love
teaches, and that, it seems, is what love is. The moral compass of the mind,
the culmination of the contest between thought and feeling, ecstasy and
contemplation, is the mental love that disposes one well toward all creation.

That stanza is love as process, but even its apparent conclusion rests on
unstable ground. To some extent the stanza's friction precludes the last line
as a simple, easy answer to its poetical convulsions, and the rest of the poem
embraces this anxiety:

But are there not some other marks that prove,
What is this wonder of the soul, call'd love?
O yes there are, but of a different kind,
The dreadful horrors of a dismal mind:
Some jealous fury throws her poison'd dart,
And rends in pieces the distracted heart. (16–21)

Paine's preemptive answer to his own question betrays the difficulty of the question as well as the answer. Coalescing around the alliterative "dreadful," "dismal," "dart," and "distraction," the love that teaches a moral of universal kindness also tears the heart and drags the mind into its most dismal states of despair. These are love's "marks," the external markers of love's presence, and like any mark they both indicate and injure, display and etch, but simultaneously enact "the simulacrum of a presence that dislocates, displaces, and refers beyond itself."[28] They drive the poem to its darkest moment:

> When love's a tyrant, and the soul a slave,
> No hope remains to thought, but in the grave;
> In that dark den it sees an end to grief,
> And what was once its dread becomes relief. (22–25)

Again emphasizing consonant heavy *d* words, Paine offers death as the comfort and alternative of the distracted heart, and again thought emerges as the truest suffering element in love. This is kindness to all in its most poisoned, perverted form; the transformation of grief to relief, magnified and ironically emphasized by the rhyme, can only understand death as a kindness, and in so doing, becomes the definitive "proof" of love as soulful "wonder." This stanza displaces all that comes before it, substituting proof (what love can teach) for proof (death as kindness in love's slavery) and transposing the notion of love's indescribability beyond feeling, and the problem of describing it to those who haven't felt it with the total embrace of that which ends all feeling. Feeling, then, is not an answer to the question.

Indeed, this eradication of feeling frees up the poem to confront the horrific reality of love as thought:

> What are the iron chains that hands have wrought?
> The hardest chain to break is made of thought.
> Think well of this, ye lovers, and be kind,
> Nor play with torture on a tortured mind. (25–29)[29]

This is the dreadful end to love as thought that has abandoned feeling of any kind. What is left is not tatters but chains, and the direct address to the lovers to "think well," no less than his preemptive answering of the question earlier in the poem, represents and reflects the dangerous, sad, and still compelling final answer to the poem's titular question. No moral rests in thought, merely the call to think "well," and universal benevolence as the genuine mark of love is distilled into mere kindness. If Paine elides the distinction between being kind and acting kindly earlier because it simply does not matter under the rubric of universal benevolence, then here he refuses the elision because it still does not matter, but for a different reason. Acting kindly is only possible in the spectrum of feeling that has forcibly disappeared in the second half of this poem, and all that is left is "play" that becomes the reiterative torture of a tortured mind. The rhyme of "kind" and "mind" is the utterly brutal last word, a poetical gesture of unity that echoes the poem's hopeful third stanza, but that betrays the intellectual torture that "what is love" is a question better not asked rather than answered at all.

SIX

Tom the Bodice-Maker

Paine in English Poetry of the 1790s

> Pure are the maxims flowing from thy pen,
> And future times will hail *thee* first of men.
> In talents *every* walk, *sublime*, or *gay*,
> *Nervous* and *clear* 'tis thine to lead the way,
> Each truth *elucidate* or Grace *display*.

> —Anonymous author, ca. 1793

A florid, celebratory poem describing Paine in language rarely applied to one of the most feared and hated men in England during the 1790s, this acrostic, taken from *A Tribute to Liberty: Or A Collection of Select Songs,* unusually celebrates Paine in the most unusual of terms. "Pure," when many of those same "maxims" were made synonymous with rape, murder, theft, and pillage; "sublime," an ironic appropriation of Edmund Burke's famous treatise, when Paine was also called "vi'prous" and, like the creature whose name that word invokes, assumed to be poisonous to peaceful social order; "nervous," when he was accused of writing feelingly and, as a former staymaker, of being overly intimate with feminine emotional states and bodies; "gay" when he was considered mad and forever scheming against king, Commons, and people; and full of grace when he was deemed, if not the brother, then certainly the son of Satan. The acrostic praises in terms directly contrary to most English poetic representations of Paine in the 1790s but, no less than those poems critical of him, represents Paine's central poetic symbolism in and value to English poetry in that decade, when he published two of his most important and legacy-creating works: *Rights of Man* and *The Age of Reason.* And while the pamphlets, prose tracts, or newspaper reports written in response to those works typically garner most critical attention, by far the most inventive, passionate, and colorful responses to Paine in the 1790s came in poetry, poetry collections, songsters, and broadsides. There is a veritable subculture if not subgenre of Paine poems written and published during the decade, on the whole a massively underrepresented body of literature in the study of Paine and the 1790s. Overwhelmingly negative and outrightly hostile to Paine's person, ideas, and legacy, these poems exist as a significant body of work that treats Paine as both the essential villain and the necessary scapegoat for any and all political change and the shifting dynamics of national identity in the period.[1] Paine is nothing less than a poetic shibboleth—"elusive phantom and material body," the spectropolitical, phantasmical oracle for republicanism and levelling, an absent actor whose absence itself was a condemnation of his vice, but also an opportunity to generate a straw man for all the social ills of England and the very real threat of the importation of French revolutionary ideals into Britain.[2] If it is indeed true that all nations are imaginary, or at least derive their hegemonic cultural coherence through imaginary bonds, then the vast majority of Paine-focused English poems in the 1790s catalogue the potential transformation of that imagination into a nightmare.

A convenient means of analyzing the largely anti-Paine corpus of poetry begins with a broadside that invokes the mythological figure of John Bull to proffer Paine as a kind of inadvertent catalyst for "real" English values and nationalism, ripping the English out of their collective stupor and arousing their latent patriotism. Entitled *John Bull Roused from his Lethargy*, the broadside happily indulges the rumors of Paine's predilection for drink.[3] However, as *John Bull Roused from his Lethargy* opens, it is John Bull who "lay[s] asleep on a Hogshead of Beer," while "A rascally Rabble, led on by Monsieur,/Laid a Plot to surprise him, and as it is said,/To drink up his Liquor, and cut off his Head" (1–4). The poetic narrator's passive construction ("it is said") exaggerates the vulnerability of John Bull, and the French honorific "Monsieur" identifies the "rascally Rabble" as French while recalling and invoking the hierarchical social levelling of the French Revolution. It is thus at once general in its application to a single man, the "monsieur" of the poem, but specific in its social implication for all men. The caesural structure of the opening stanza's last line reinforces that very relationship first suggested by "monsieur"; the drinking up of liquor is both a generalized stereotype of French predilections as well as an action identifiable with John Bull himself, while the cutting off of his head is nothing less than the symbolic act of the revolution itself.

Set to the tune of "Derry Down," a patriotic song celebrating British liberty written by none other than George Alexander Stevens, this poem has Paine ask the patriotically provocative question: "What Business has John/To that Cask of October he's snoring upon?" (5–6). A clearly identified "Tom Paine" allied to but contrasted with the relatively anonymous Monsieur introduces the poem's only named figure other than John Bull. By questioning John Bull's ownership of and rights to the "cask," the poet invokes the common criticism of Paine's *Rights of Man*, namely that it advocated outright theft, but also embeds a criticism of John Bull within the criticism of Paine. John Bull is blissfully unaware of what is going on, and practically, if not formally, insists on his "Cask of October" being stolen because of his willingly induced soporific ignorance. Monsieur's response, "Vat John Business? Him Business echoed Monsieur—/ You and I, Monsieur Paine equal Right to the de Beer" (7–8), mistakes Bull for business and indicts them both, as Monsieur sees the proclamation and exertion of his "equal Right to de beer" as his own very business, which, given the poem's identification of beer with Bull, is nothing less than the theft of Bull's own national identity: a patriotic coup d'état.

This confluence and compression of identity and act energizes and enables the cascade effect of Paine's call to rights. When you have a "right to de beer" you also have a right to everything else owned by John Bull:

> Notres Jacobine Gentlemen too is ver plain—
> Equal Right to John's Bullocks, John's Mutton, and Grain;
> John's October sans Doute for me verily tink—
> Good Liquor may tempt e'en Dissenters to drink. (9–12)

If the opening stanzas operate by compression, namely a conflation of personal and national identity through both the specific and the general, then this third of six stanzas operates by both substitution and allusion. "John" has become a placeholder, the generic term for the English everyman who loses his identity prior to having it stolen. What the "jacobine gentlemen" have a right to is structured as a series of contested possessives, and that the first two terms are imaginatively linked to bulls—bullocks and mutton—highlights the fact that John here is absent his Bull.[4] John's grain then catches the rabble's eye, as had a grain alcohol product at poem's start. Each is a shifting signifier trying to fill a gap, generate relationship, and establish national identity when it is most tenuous and liable to be appropriated by the rabble. Each is a significant material object related to the poem's constituent components of John Bull's national identity and equally a consumable product that Paine, Monsieur, and the rabble see not as material signifiers of national identity but rather as their rights and, as rights, objects they are obligated to obtain and, in obtaining, define.

This tantalizing brew of materialism, nationalism, identity, and rights marks the halfway point of the poem, which shifts focus slightly to the English response, not from the still incapacitated John Bull but from an anonymous English Tar, thus inverting and echoing the nominal structure of the rabble, Paine, and Monsieur. The sailor opens with a significant play on words:

> You a right? cried a Tar, who stepd'd in unobserv'd—
> You a right Ragamuffins, you ought to be starv'd—
> What drink up his Stingo, and quarter his Sheep—
> Steal his Cattle and Grain, while the Fellow's asleep? (13–16)

Bookended by questions, and emphasized by the his use of "ragamuffin," the tar's matter of fact astonishment at what Paine and the French rabble had essayed—drink, quarter, and steal—works both to demystify and depersonalize those objects as constituent parts of John Bull's identity and transform them into things that define Paine, Monsieur, and the rabble as thieves no matter their rights. This explains the play on "rights" in the opening two lines of the stanza. The sailor "steps in unobserv'd" and cries "You a right?," which is at once a statement and symbolic gesture of enduring community and fraternal bonds between Englishmen ([Are] you a[ll] right?) and also a characteristic fusion of rights theory and self and national identity in the poem—"You a right" sounds like the tar is asking Paine, Monsieur, and the rabble if they think of themselves *as* rights, thereby asserting their theft as the very action which defines the source and summit of their identity: they are nothing but thieves. The echo a line later ("You a right Ragamuffins") strengthens and consolidates that vision of identity, as the tar decides that both the act and the identity is that of the ragamuffian assertion of their moral failings within the context of the tar's defense of his genuine rights.

This is the defining moment of the broadside, where competing linguistic measures mark essentializing political, moral, and social differences, and as the final, sixth stanza is merely a toast, it is the subsequent fifth stanza that brings the poem to its violent end:

> Split my Timbers I'll rouse him—then give him a Shake,
> John sprung on his Legs and was quickly awake;
> Grasp'd his good oaken Cudgell, prepar'd for the War,
> Kick'd Tom Paine, bang'd Monsieur, and rewarded the Tar. (17–20)

A series of internal connections cohere around John Bull's revival and assured survival and Paine's ironic, unwitting arousal of John Bull. He is again merely "John" here, but what takes the place of his name as a form of identity is what this poem all along insists is identity's necessary twin: action. Violence offers Paine as the special embodiment of a Focualdian notion— "From being an art of unbearable sensations, punishment has become an economy of suspended rights"—in that here, the unbearable sensations are exactly what suspend his questionable rights.[5] The shifting measures of verb time are crucial. First comes future tense in the Tar's proclamation (I will rouse him), then past tense becomes a perfect emblem of England at the moment, since it is tradition and the past, constitutions and monarchies, that constituted the bulk of opposition to Paine. These shifting tenses are shaped by the precise unfolding of events in the stanza, as John is "sprung," "grasp'd," and "prepare'd," then "kicks," "bangs," and "rewards." He duly wields an oaken cudgel, long standing symbol of the British monarchy, but the two-line stretch over which he "springs," "grasps," and "prepares" temporarily delays while the deployment of verbs in the last verse, "kicks," "bangs," and "rewards," are unleashed in an energetic torrent, in parallel to and yet slightly askew from the other forms of preparation in the stanza. There is a strange harmony to this stanza, a relish in the destruction, and although unstated, an idea nonetheless lingers—that Paine, Monsieur, and the rabble will have coming to them what really is their right: pain and punishment, the worst of "unbearable sensations."

A similar attitude but different approach is taken in another broadside, *The British Lyon Rous'd; Or, John Bull For Ever.*[6] Opening with the fabulist "The Fox has lost his tail./The Ass has done his Braying./ The Devil has got Tom Paine," the poem evokes a commonplace constructed by Paine's poetic opponents: his intimate relationship with Satan.[7] This poem does so by promising Paine that "If long in [Satan's] service he hop'd to remain,/He must seize the roast beef of Old England,/Seize all the English Roast Beef" (3–5). Satan offers Paine an object no less material and consumable than his grain and bullocks: roast beef. The poem contends that as long as the roast beef is "in the land/John Bull would be able his foes to withstand" (6–7), and the manner the poem suggests for Satan (and Paine) to take the roast beef is in its living form of the "fat ox" (11). That "fat ox" is set up against Paine's fable character of the Ass, who

> soon trump'd up a scurrilous plan,
> By which our fat oxen he thought to trepan,
> So he wrote to JOHN BULL what he calls *Rights of Man*
> Which lost him roast beef of old England. (16–20)

Paine's words are cast as pure torture, medically gruesome attempts at directly accessing the brains of Englishmen, but to little or no effect. What is thus lost in the procedure is not a patient but the heart and mind of the English nation.

While the devil and Paine subsequently run to France, the poem suggests that "Could the Fox and the Ass but have level'd the land,/With our good British beef their own guts they have cramm'd" (26–27). The visceral consumption of roast beef renders Paine's work in France as the opposite of his work in and on Britain: if trepanning is to remove and relieve through legitimized torture, then cramming is to increase by unfettered and willful consumption. But somewhere between trepanning and cramming lies the moral of this fable:

> Now the moral is clear, and you all understand,
> May the King, like a Lion, defend our good land,
> May the Fox lose his tail, and Paine be hang'd
> And we eat roast beef in old England. (36–39)

The act that coheres the English into a people is neither political nor consumable per se; it is a product rendered consumable in a refined and communal way, transformed into an Anglican Eucharistic moment where the shared consumption, act as much as object, builds community and reinforces shared national beliefs that ironically culminate in another form of torture, here state-sanctioned: hanging.

Paine's satanic relationships are explored differently in Samuel Ashby's *Miscellaneous Poems.*[8] His first and longest poem, "The Illustrious Friends," is crafted as a dialogue and begins by calling Paine "Sedition's chief, illustrious Paine" (7) and "great Legislator Paine!" (15) who addresses Satan:

> Dread sire! I'm mighty glad, to find
> I've done *this* mission to *your* mind!
> 'Tis true, I try'd to act *your* part,
> And had *your* interest *most* at heart;
> Much I enforc'd *your* grand design,
> The Democratic scheme *divine!*

> *I* taught the *equalizing* plan,
> And *thus* proclaim'd the Rights of Man! (25–32)

If later images will render Paine as a demon, this shows Paine "acting" like Satan, simulating and reenacting his own imagined pantomime of Satan's mindful intentions but also his interested heart. This synchrony between Satan's logical and affective desires is expressed in the poem as rigidly systematic forms, which are at once externally imposed, artificial political strictures, diabolically represented as natural liberties and rights in *Rights of Man*, as well as the forms the application of those strictures as liberties take. "Design," "scheme," and "plan" frame the systematic, intentional, and ultimately disorienting nature of Paine's political ideals, while Paine himself casts the success of those ideals as demonically serendipitous despite the intentionality behind them, whose only and ultimate aim is to foster his relationship with Satan. Content "to find" that he has completed a "mission" that meets Satan's "mind," with his interest at "heart," there is an emotional plea here for Satan to accept the value and success of Paine's "try." That "try" in turn is counterpoised by Paine's "teaching," which renders as equal all sociopolitical power but does so only through the initial inequality between the pleading Paine and the listening Satan.

Paine can only resolve this interpersonal disorder by evoking the very group—the people—who are affected by the "equalizing plan," which is as much a description of his attempts at relating to Satan as it is of his politics. Not only does "all power come from the People,—then / All power reverts to them *again*" (33), but "*power* and *right* are just the *same*, / And differ, *merely* in the *name*" (41–42). Who, then, are these people into whom Paine divests his rights? "Who are the People? I reply, / The *Mob*, the *Party*—*You* and *I*" (47–48). The collective people are reduced down to the most basic of social dyads, you and I, and in that dyad Paine finds the relationship and connection he yearns for with Satan. More than proxies, the people constitute the very substance of his equalizing plan. They function as an indistinguishable part of Paine's identity. This is precisely why the laws, transformed by Paine's design in *Rights of Man*,

> which *should* a nation bind,
> Must know the *Individual* mind;
>
> . . . .
>
> For if you miss a *single* soul,
> The laws are *vague*, and void the *whole*:
> And *thus* I made it clearly known,
> That *every* Man should make *his own*. (49–50, 53–56)

Desperate not merely to act like Satan but to be Satan, Paine leverages the laws to maximize individual desire over collective good as long as they mimic Paine as Paine has Satan: by "knowing the individual mind." This kind of political telepathy, which disregards the common good of the rule of law, pointedly demonstrates why

> Man! spite of *metaphysic* prate,
> Is form'd an *independent State;*
> Containing, in his very *nature,*
> *All* principles of *legislature;*
> Responsible, and bound to *none;*
> A pure *Democracy,* in *One.* (83–88)

The radical individualism of Paine's scheme grinds the oscillating tensions of his speech to a halt. Subsumed into the "democracy of one," which claims political priority for, and only for, the self, such claims reflect Paine's ultimate insight into human nature: his *Rights of Man* makes claims for all, depends upon the radically individual, but ultimately binds to none.

Although the rest of the poem catalogues a Miltonic description of Satan's fall, there remains Paine's hope to bind himself to Satan as intensely as his political ideals demand being bound to none. This occurs in suitably dramatic fashion:

> I choose thee *mine,* from *all* of *Men.*
> Hence, did my bosom's *grand design,*
> By sacred influx, burn in *thine!*
> Influx divine! whole subtle flame,
> Transfus'd *my* spirit, thro' *thy* frame,
> Temper'd like *mine,* thy *pliant* heart;
> And steel'd thee for thy Satan's *part!* (163–69)

A crucial trinity of words baptize Paine as Satan's simulacrum: "influx," "transfus'd," and "temper'd." Each suggests a measured commixture of elements—spirit, blood, and metal—and so Satan's dramatic selection of Paine is offered not so much as a taking over of his body as it is a recognition of his preexisting likeness; Paine has already infused Satan into his "pliant heart," an affective act of comingling, achieved already but here verified through an act whose strength is also a pun on its greatest and only political claim: steeling/stealing.

This potent combination of demonic influences and affective union takes a decidedly different turn in a Christmas-themed broadside from 1792. *A Christmas Box, for the Republicans* takes its name from a traditional box in which Christmas donations are put, often until it is filled to breaking.[9] Invoking the Devil initially, who with "democrats" and "gallic knaves," "under *Freedom's* specious mask, combine to make us slaves" (1–2), the poem casts Satan on the side of the equalizing rogues who seek to steal what belongs rightfully to Britons, but it shifts the focus from Paine's desire for union with Satan to his staymaking past. While the poem's opening five stanzas trace over the minute details of revolutionary fantasy, only to "find delightful golden dreams, all terminate in ruin" (20), the poem's middle portion (stanzas 6–12) is dedicated exclusively to Paine, offered as the paradigmatic "equalizing rogue" who

> was born a shabby dog, by trade a *lousy tailor*,
> His goose and bodkin he forsook, and ran away from jail, sir;
> He left off stitching woman's stays, and statesman did commence, sir,
> He wrote to tickle *asses* ears and called it "COMMON SENSE," sir. (21–24)

The poem reads Paine's early life as a staymaker as a kind of perverse training for his presumptive "statesmanship" and his abandonment of that career as the model for his fugitive movements away from British justice.[10] Paine's *Common Sense* is the rehearsal for his ultimate demonic role, as

> The *Devil* pleas'd with what *Tom* wrote, engaged him as his *clerk*, sir,
> And with *his Tommy* did cajole, and mutter in the dark, sir;
> To raise the *tailor* from his board, the devil form'd a plan, sir,
> And bid the cross'leg'd knave compose, his cursed "RIGHTS OF MAN," sir. (25–28)

A "low word" according to Samuel Johnson, "cajole" segues into the image of a cross-legged Paine, which, like the earlier image of him stitching women's stays, aims to discredit and undermine Paine's masculinity and decry his political promiscuity as a linked disability.[11]

A Christmas Box echoes a number of 1790s poems that suggested Paine's staymaking past effeminized him, fed into his sexual lechery, and made his argument for democracy unmanly and his demand for rights in the body politic no different than claiming a female body as his own. In another Christmas poem, *A Word to the Wise; or, Old England for ever,* published as a broadside in 1792, Paine's proximity to women is read as an enjoyment in measuring women so intense that "E'en our Wives and our Daughters

tho' deucedly vain,/In Old England shall scorn to be *laced* by Tom Paine"
(21–22). Another broadside from the same year, *Tom the Bodice Maker,* contends that

> From moulding forms, and bolst'ring shapes, he's turn'd to shaping
> laws, Sir,
> To enlarge Old English freedom, and revive the GOOD OLD CAUSE, Sir,
> With store of *Noncons* at his beck, and many a politic raker
> Who hourly rave, "Save us, sweet Tom!—dear Tom the *Bodice-Maker.*"
> (12–15)

Crafting restricting garments as much as restrictive political ideas, effeminized and hypersexualized, Paine's assumptive move from women's bodies
to the body politic, from the shape of women to the rights of man, is offered
as a calibrated aberration and deviation from normative masculine sexuality.
   These deviations explain why, as *A Christmas Box* accuses,

> He wrote so *feelingly* to knaves, whose pockets were quite empty,
> That proselytes he soon obtain'd, full nineteen out of twenty;
> He found the *villains* were all ripe, to massacre the great, sir,
> Like *cannibals* they drank their blood, and human flesh they eat, sir.
> (33–36)

The feminized Paine writes "feelingly," appealing to the inherently violent
emotional tendencies of his audience and so exciting social passions to such
an extent that he exacerbates an already impassioned set of proselytes to
massacre and murder.[12] In "A Parody of Anacreon to Heaven," found in
Gower's Patriotic Songster, these same cannibal proselytes with "transports of
joy/Away to Tom Paine [did] instantly fly" (15–16), and upon arrival Paine
proclaims, "I'll lend you my thimble, my bodkin, and shears" (7). Here
Paine attracts the transported, and the tools of his staymaking trade have
become the weapons of revolution, which he will "'lend" and not give. In *A
Christmas Box,* the common people are "ripe" for their cannibalism, attuned
to the overwrought emotionality of Paine's writing and gleefully indulging
the self-destructive nature of their passions—a cannibalism that preys on
fear but is the necessary consequence of excessive feminized feeling, insistently a perversion of their perceived role in the domestic sphere.[13] *The Life
and Character of Mr. Thomas Paine,* a 1793 broadside also included in *Gower's
Patriotic Songster,* viscerally explores this: "The stays so slim,/And bodice
trim,/[Paine's] fingers light discover" (13–15). The poem's version of Paine
goes on to write *Rights of Man* in order

T'improve the murd'ring art:
Lamp-chords were strung
With bodies hung,
And women eat the heart. (57–60)

Women and their cannibalistic and thus self-consuming tendencies are immoral exemplars of Paine's political ideals, and the feminized Paine exults in the worst sociopolitical consequence of his writing because it perverts both natural and political ideals.

This excessive emotional appeal on Paine's part makes the narrator of *A Christmas Box* wish that "on some lofty gibbet hung" those "who from the *truth* depart" (42), for only then "*Tom Paine* his dirty jobs would lose, and no employment find, sir" (44). The return to the professional context of Paine's political thought and social agitation denudes and disrupts the excessive feeling with which he writes. Indeed, as the poem tries to show, the deep, destructive irony of Paine's "feeling" is that within himself it is inauthentic, merely a function of his lecherous employment. Function, not feeling, is Paine's vice. And while he does not himself feel, he agitates and stirs in the English, and most damningly in women, a mode of self-consumption that is viscerally destructive because genuinely felt. The narrator of *A Christmas Box* sees this disparity between Paine's inauthentic and his subject's authentic feelings as a function of his sexuality: "*Tom Paine* may like a monkey grin, but *Tom* shall not prevail, sir,/The *British Lion* ne'er will run, from *pricklouse Tom the Tailor*" (47–48). While the rest of the poem goes on to celebrate the British Lion's trade and commerce, these terminal lines on Paine's role in social upheaval and rejuvenating an English national sensibility again draw on a criticism of Paine's employment to assert his failure at such upheavals. "The Lion and the Pricklouse" suggests an Aesopian fable whose moral is that authentic belief trumps the mere employment and deployment of feeling, but "pricklouse," with its history as a derogatory term for tailors, draws together the images and themes of the poem's "interpretation" of Paine. "Pricklouse" is an echo of the poem's first description of Paine as a "lousy" tailor, both terrible at his job and comparable to a louse. The suggestion of a little prick is of course a reference to the injuries a tailor's customer might sustain, as well as the blood drawn, certainly appealing to a cannibal. Yet with a cross-legged Paine who writes feelingly, thus appealing to the lowest order of human thought and action, if not a categorically different one, it is not beyond the pale to consider that pricklouse Tom the Tailor is so because he is bad at his job, but likewise because he has a louse-sized prick.

Another poem from *Gower's Patriotic Songster,* "Tom Paine's Vision," offers an elegiac, meditative, and somewhat fantastical and gothic take on Paine's inherent capacity to aberrantly incite feelings in himself and others:

> The clock struck twelve when TOM PAINE wake'd to view
> A *grimly smiling specter* by his side—
> Fear shook his limbs, which all with cold sweat ran,
> And rais'd his hair-when thus the shade began. (7–10)

Having horrified Paine and thrust him into an agitated state, the supernatural visitor informs him of his purpose: "From realms infernal, lo! I come/T'adopt thee Pluto's darling son" (11–12). Substituting the mythological god of the underworld for Satan, the poem grants Paine a newfound kinship that is the result of a specifically affective act:

> Aghast all we infernals stood,
> While France was reeking in her blood,
> And almost pity felt!
> But soon rejoiced we were to see
> *Thy* bosom heave with extacy,
> While massacres were dealt. (17–22)

Paine's decision to support the French Revolution is a sentimental one, that which develops in him an ecstasy that inversely and proportionately parallels the gods' own pity. It simultaneously renders Paine's deeply felt, affective response not simply as the perverse consequence of his own arguments for sympathy as a political value in *Common Sense,* but as a basic, vicious act of detachment of the feeling from the one for whom the feeling is felt.[14] Here, unlike in many other poems that cast Paine as teacher and the public as his pupils, it is not Paine's diabolical ability to make people think like him that is his most seditious quality. It is his near supernatural ability to make others feel the same way he does.[15]

"The Physician and the Patients," from the same collection, suggests a novel cause for Paine's special affectiveness:

> Dame Discord grown tir'd of her own native hell,
> Made a trip up to earth, as our histories tell;
> On ruin determin'd—as loyalty's bane,
> Took a stay-makers' form, and she call'd herself *Paine.* (1–4)

Paine's lecherous proximity to women and pitiful masculine endowment as staymaker reaches its logical end: he becomes a woman, or, rather, a woman becomes him. With Paine the feminized vehicle for her spirit, his works become the vehicles for her discord. While *"America* foster'd her malice at first" (5), it is "With vexation and spite, swift to Britain she flew" (7–8), and

> There she wrote and she rav'd on all manner of things,
> And kick'd at all order—*Lords, Commons,* and *Kings;*
> Like a whore she entic'd, and some fools at her ran,
> She infected them all with her curs'd *Rights of Man.* (9–12)

Of all the criticism leveled at him, never before was Paine cast as a whore, nor *Rights of Man* as a sexually transmitted disease, which as the poem continues "threaten'd each dupe with a total decay." It will take "old Doctor Government" to remedy and halt the spread of the disease, but the damage is already done, scar tissue from the sexualized encounter. Indeed, as the poem ends, Discord "perceives" British resistance to her sexual advances, and irresistible to check, *"Bloody France* my successes shall tell,/And her rabble out-do all the daemons of hell" (31–32). The rendering of Paine as whore and his works as sexual infection reaches its logical end here too; with France already in the thrall of the feminized Paine, those infected will proclaim Paine's success in such a way that "democracy appears as a brazen whore," because what it spreads is a virulent strain of Paine's *Rights of Man.*[16]

My concern in this chapter has largely been with grassroots and minor poets whose gripes with Paine responded to the vacuum created by his absence from England. However, the most prominent representation of Paine in poetry, which occurs in the works of Peter Pindar, alias of John Wolcott, considers that absence as the very force of his influence. His two odes to Thomas Paine, published in 1791, are the most prominent examples of Paine-focused poetry in the period, and begin with a unique take on the familiar poetic strategy of relating Paine to mythological figures:

> O PAINE! thy vast endeavor I admire!
> How brave the hope to set a realm on fire!—
> AMBITION smiling prais'd thy giant wish:
> Compared to *thee,* the MAN, to gain a name,
> Who to DIANA's temple put the flame,
> A simple minnow to the KING OF FISH. (1–6)[17]

The opening stanza wonderfully plays with the size of the ego behind Paine's ambition. Both "vast" and "giant," ambition connects Paine to the appropriately unnamed Herostratus, the fourth-century criminal who set fire to Diana's temple in an effort to become famous. As punishment, it was forbidden for anyone to say or speak his name. Pindar leverages the ode tradition of the address to pointedly show how futile and egotistically self-serving Paine's attempts at political change—setting the realm on fire—really are. The address, "O PAINE," figures the named Paine as the poem's addressee but compares him to the unnamed Herostratus, whose punishment is to be wiped from all human thought and memory as punishment for his hopes for immortal fame. By comparing the named Paine to the unnamed but alluded to Herostratus, Pindar suggests the paradox at the heart of Paine's ambition: its end is only to make him famous and not to initiate legitimate social and political change as claimed, yet it will eventually relegate Paine to the rubbish bin of remembrance and memory.

Thus Paine is the king of fish, another mythological reference to the Greek god Triton who stilled, and did not rouse, the waves. The degree to which Paine differs is simply a matter of his to-be-named ambition:

Oh, must the scythe of DESOLATION sleep,
So keen for carnage, stay its mighty sweep,
And HAVOCK on his hunter drop his lash;
Spurr'd, arm'd, and ripe to storm with groans the sky,
To chase an empire, and enjoy the cry,
The cry of millions—what a glorious crash! (13–18)

The paradoxical energy of the poem initiated by the opening stanza plays upon the activation of havoc in these lines. At once meaning "massive destruction" and also "plunder and taking," havoc here supersedes mere desolation, which merely "sleeps."[18] If desolation means utter annihilation, then that, as Pindar points out, is not what Paine aims for: his ambition is not to obliterate. Instead his goal is havoc: the more socially oriented, less totalitarian chaos of large scale but not complete destruction, and likewise the plunder, theft, and pillaging that Paine poetry often invokes as his true aim in *Rights of Man*. Only then could Paine invert the typical power dyad of empire and make empire the chased and the hunted—a victim, and not an agent of Paine's sociopolitical havoc.

This perverse inversion explains "How DEATH had grinn'd delight, and Hell been glad,/To see our liberties o'erturning" (18–19). "O'erturning" is here a political action borne of Paine's havoc, and the poem goes on to catalogue the remainder of those actions:

Why, cur-like, didst thou sneak away, nay fly?
Dread'st thou of anger'd JUSTICE the sharp eye?

Return, and bring MESDAMES POISSARDES along:
And lo, with FRIENDSHIP's squeeze and fire to meet 'em,
And oaths of ev'ry hue to greet 'em,
The sisterhood of Billingsgate shall throng. (25–30)

It has been suggested that "the radical writer's audience bore resemblance to the eighteenth-century crowd, the riotous mob," and here Pindar imagines that crowd as exclusively female.[19] The stanza operates on two linked images and movements: sneaking and returning. The gradual, casual insistence of Paine's flight, as "sneak[ing] away, nay fly[ing]," casts the flight as one of cowardice more than criminality, and as such the return is characterized more by Paine's company than Paine himself: Madame Poissardes and the market women of France who, in the 1789 March of Versailles, marched against high food prices and thus initiated one of the vital precursors to the French Revolution. This is yet another—though far more subtle and devastating—representation of feminized Paine, since Paine's act is read not as cowardice but, like the March of Versailles, a preliminary act of social unrest and upheaval, havoc actualized, aiming to disrupt the social cohesion of England without desolating it. In the subsequent stanza, Pindar suggests that "PAINE, GORDON, and REBELLION, shall shake hands" (36), but here the force and consequence of this social disruption embedded in Paine's connection to women is focused not on a genteel handshake but another form of affective social communication: "Friendship's squeeze."[20] The phrase initially reads like a form of intra-feminine intimacy and thus of community and relationship. Yet the meaning of squeeze interferes with the notion of friendship that proceeds it, since squeeze means both "an application of strong and heavy pressure" and "the pressure of a crowd of persons; a crush."[21] Friendship's squeeze is therefore not a form of community building but of social violence—the application of pressure and force, specifically from outside, in an attempt to compress, crush, and "o'erturn." This is exactly why "The sisterhood of Billingsgate shall throng." Pindar locates in "sisterhood" the greatest threat to England's social order; Paine's ability to arouse women's passions represents a vital instigation of social violence as political change, summing up their physical, political, and ideological threat as "thronging." Pindar's "Ode II" will call Paine's followers the "democratic throng," but here, understood as both object and action, noun and verb, "throng" in Pindar's poetical grammar means to "press; compress, force in a crowd," but must mean "to cohere into a crowd" in the context of the stanza's attempts to cast not just women in the abstract but crowds of women as transgressively dangerous. When women form crowds they are compelled by necessity to exert force and violence; they inherently represent the collective intention to "squeeze" England at the behest of Paine but also in paradoxical contrast to Paine, who sneaks and flies in order to return and squeeze. What connects this apparent paradox is the fact that the women are Billingsgate women. It is England's largest fish market. Paine is truly the king of fish: he is a "cur," not a dog as one might expect but a fish native to the British Isles.[22] Paine "sneaks" and "flies" like a fish, he returns with a woman whose name literally means "fishwife," and together they stir the fish-women of Billingsgate to "squeeze" and "throng." There is for Pindar undoubtedly something fishy going on.

Pindar's riposte against Paine is emblematic of the spectropolitcal anxieties about Paine's absence from England, but so too was the poetic response to Pindar: "The Melancholy Catastrophe, or, A Peep into Bethlehem," by Peter Fig. Taking up Pindar's fascination with the sisterhood of Billingsgate, Fig casts them as the mournful chorus lamenting Pindar's failures:

> SISTERS of Billingsgate the lay begin;
> Let mournful clamors howl thro' every lane:
> Nymphs of St. Giles, ah! cease to quaff your gin;
> Break; break, your pipes, and join the mournful strain. (1–4)

Those failures paint Pindar not as the "king" of fish but "Prince of grub street meter" (5), and after a fable in which the "whale" Pindar is described as the frog who wished to be an ox and his sycophancy to George III painted as writing "'gainst liberty, but call[ing] it loyal" (30), Fig then gets to the heart of Pindar's poetic viciousness:

> Well did'st thou sing, how Peggy, frantic dame,
> Was disappointed in her aim;
> How may fools the rash attempt invites:
> Then themes congenial swell'd thy humourous song.
> How female madness rais'd a sneaking throng. (37–41)

Condensing Paine's movements in Pindar's first ode into the simultaneous crowd formation and pressure exerting of "throng," Fig locates the real if unspoken anxiety revealed by Pindar's criticism: female madness and its potential for creating and sustaining social disorder. "Frantic" and "disappointed," Peggy is the poem's very "melancholy catastrophe," she who becomes the punch line to Pindar's comedic poems, but whose ability to cohere franticness and disappointment into the single state of madness perfectly embodies the meaning and import of Paine's ideas to the English.

Such cohesion inevitably leads one to Bedlam, and it is the second of Fig's odes that offers the titular "peep" into that institution. Demanding that Pindar "let Paine alone" (1) and arguing that "Paine, supported by his cause shall stand,/The boast of this enlightened land:/the boast of liberty" (4–6), Fig soon sees that "animated themes like these,/Demand the efforts of a prouder lyre" (25–26), and he descends "to Billingsgate again" (30). This Billingsgate-as-Bedlam image embeds the female potential for social unrest in the very scope of their madness, a product as much as a cause, and Pindar soon finds himself with company in Billingsgate as Bedlam:

> Ah! then dismounted from his spavin'd hack.
> To Bethlehem's Walls with B***e I saw him borne.
> There the strait waistcoat close embrac'd his back;
> While Peggy's wreath of straw did either brow adorn;
> And there they sat; two grinners, vis-a-vis:
> He writing Grub-street verse; B***e ranting rhapsody. (73–78)

The appearance of Paine's opponent Burke, the writer to whom *Rights of Man* was a response, makes complete sense here at the end, not so much because he holds the diametrically opposed views to Paine but because, "vis-a-vis," face to face, in an intimacy reflecting their shared ideological stances, Pindar writes while Burke rants rhapsody. Leveraging a lingering sense of rhapsody as "literary work consisting of miscellaneous or disconnected pieces; a written composition having no fixed form or plan," Burke's rants are not simply incoherent, they are disconnected, no different than how female madness is represented through its coterminous franticness and disappointment.[23] Burke's ideas are thus presented as having the same deleterious effect as Paine's do in many of the poems discussed in this chapter. This is an effective retort to the collective suggestions that Paine unduly influences the thoughts and feelings of his readers on sociopolitical matters, and it is fittingly Peggy who returns, a spectral figure of female madness that looms in the background of Burke and Pindar's conference. While Pindar's cloistered waistcoat suggests that this is no more "friendship's squeeze" than is Madame Poissarde's, Peggy's straw "did either brow adorn." The casual intentionality of "adorn," but also the image of her wearing it lightly, contrasts with both the staymaking cinctures of Pindar and the fragmented ranting of Burke. This then is the image of female madness, which stands

apart from the masculine intimacy shared by Burke and Pindar, but necessarily so. Such female madness had for Pindar emblematized the deep
social risks of Paine's thought and the prurient ends of his ambition, and for
many of the poems that opposed him in the 1790s, the very affective aspect
of women to which Paine most appealed. In Fig's poem, Peggy's separation
from Pindar and Burke in her madness is deliberate but meaningful, the
very essence of the political notions that Paine had written about. No less
than the Paine presented and represented in the collective poetry written
about him in the 1790s, Peggy is spectral, a ghost of politics, an adornment
as much as the straw upon her brow.

SEVEN

The Manly Page

Philip Freneau's Poetic Affinities

There seems to be some feeling among a number of the residents of
Mount Pleasant about the change of the name of their place to Freneau. Philip Freneau, they say, and claim that the old men who knew
the man verify the assertion, was an infidel, a votary, and associate
of the notorious Tom Paine.

—"Don't Like the Name Freneau,"
Matawan Journal, Saturday, July 20, 1889

Even in the domestic politics of small-town New Jersey, a half-century
after his death, Philip Freneau could not shake an association with the
"notorious" Tom Paine. Freneau would not have wanted to do so anyway.
While often seen as an American romantic, Freneau inspires conflicting
and contradictory assessments from critics, yet when it comes to his poetical relationship to Thomas Paine, there is little room for considerations
of difference. His early poetry, especially "The Rising Glory of America,"
is deeply sympathetic to Paine's arguments for American independence in
Common Sense. But the figures who populate those poems are the dominant
personalities of the Revolution, like George Washington and John Adams,
in a process Jean Béranger calls "héroïsation," or the rendering of these figures as heroes of their professional fields and endeavors, be they political or
military.[1] Not until the politically volatile 1790s, when Paine was in France,
revolution was brewing, and Freneau took on a series of newspaper edi-
torships at no less than four newspapers across three states, did Paine became a vitally important poetic figure for Freneau. He did so as a political
thinker embodying many of Freneau's own political views and representing
the progressive surge that would guarantee human rights were defended and

monarchies abolished. In short, unlike any other of those "heroes," Paine is a hero of the American and French Revolutions as well as literature, politics, and religion for Freneau. In poems like "To The Public" and "To the Author," Paine shapes Freneau's fluid definition of authorship in turbulent political times, and in poems such as "On the Demolition of the French Monarchy," "To a Republican, With Mr. Paine's Rights of Man," and "Stanzas on the Decease of Thomas Paine," Paine becomes the heroic revolutionary singlehandedly heralding the age of reason and the downfall of kings. Paine becomes nothing short of a transcendent hero whose own pivotal role in global politics and Freneau's poetics shapes, as the people of Mount Pleasant knew, Freneau's literary legacy as much as Paine's political one.

Freneau's early poetry reflects Paine not necessarily as heroic counterpart but as a political ally who shares the same view of America and its raw potential. "The Rising Glory of America," Freneau's coauthored valedictory address to the College of New Jersey Class of 1771, which included himself, Hugh Henry Breckenridge (his coauthor), and James Madison, was a work in which "Freneau rehearsed stories that would be crucial to the prospective national identity of these future politicians and mythmakers," and in so doing framed such an expression of national identity on many of the same terms Paine did.[2] One exchange in the poetical dialogue is especially telling. After one of the speakers, Acasto, proclaims, "I see, I see / Freedom's established reign; cities, and men, / Numerous as sands upon the ocean shore" (351–53), his interlocutors caution him:

Eugenio: Nor shall these angry tumults here subside
Nor murder cease, through all these provinces,
Till foreign crowns have vanished from our view
And dazzle here no more—no more presume
To awe the spirit of fair Liberty;—
Vengeance must cut the thread,—and Britain, sure
Will curse her fatal obstinacy for it! (372–78)

After recounting a litany of British abuses against America and Americans, Eugenio is answered by Leander:

Here independent power shall hold her sway,
And public virtue warm the patriot breast:
No traces shall remain of tyranny,
And laws, a pattern to the world beside,
Be here enacted first. (431–35)

Aggressive British military acts and political policies have, in Eugenio's mind, voided any English monarchical claims to America, and its "presumption" to terrorize the native American "spirit of Liberty" demands a single response from Americans: vengeance. That is itself a particularly aggressive if justified response in Eugenio's mind, and Leander's retort is meant both to contain that aggression and to offer an equally forceful alternative. For him, the current answer to past British violence is "sway," a notion that encompasses a prevailing influence, here political in nature, but also motion and movement, a physical distancing from British influence and not so much a dissociated "cut thread" of vengeance—a pendulum swing away from reliance on Britain and not a gravitational drop.[3] Public virtue here seems more than the sum of its parts, certainly valor, strength, and courage, but also something that, given its direct relationship to "sway" in the poem, acts upon what all swaying needs: a source of movement. The success of "independent power" relies on the political disposition of the people but also on the public exercise of seeking and achieving independence, which is the very "public virtue" that can "warm the patriot breast." The cumulative effect of the sweeping motion of independent power and the creeping warmth of public virtue is erasure: "no traces" of tyranny will remain. This total eradication of tyranny is not as putatively violent as vengeance, but it is no less total in its ends. This enlightened alternative to pure vengeance, a wiping away as opposed to a cutting, is predicated on the "laws, a pattern to the world beside," which are "here enacted first." The echo of "here" resonates as both the realm of "independent sway" and the originary location from which all laws opposing tyranny radiate, as does tyranny's antidote: patterning. Tyranny recedes into nothing, the law extends outward into the "world," not self-contained but self-replicating and so specific as to not merely be "here" but "beside."

What distinguishes Paine's *Common Sense* from Freneau's poem, however, is Paine's emphasis on the formation of government as a privileged instrument for the very public virtue Freneau writes about: "Here then is the origin and rise of government; namely, a mode rendered necessary by the inability of moral virtue to govern the world; here too is the design and end of government; viz. freedom and security. And however our eyes may be dazzled with show, or our ears deceived by sound; however prejudice will warp our wills, or interest darken our understanding, the simple voice of nature and reason will say 'tis right."[4] In Paine's appeal to "nature and reason" lies part of that public virtue so crucial to Freneau. In the broad strokes Paine's and Freneau's arguments are deeply sympathetic, with the function of government for Paine, namely freedom and security, being specific formulations of the bounds of Freneau's "sway" and the coherent structure of the law's pattern in "The Rising Glory of America." Despite their obvious attractions, the danger of such laws as opponents of tyranny and monarchy lies in a very specific and unique shared term for both Freneau and Paine: dazzle.

For Freneau "dazzle" is the defining action of foreign crowns, the strange yet untenable attraction of monarchy to a populace, and likewise monarchy's ability to overwhelm and diminish the political will and mental capacities of its subjects. The force of this attraction is so total that the only solution for Freneau, espoused by Eugenio, is for it to vanish—either to exist or not, not to exist in half measures and less than completely. The vanishing of the crown is not simply its political rejection nor its relegation to another shore. It is its utter annihilation. For Paine, "dazzle" is the consequence of monarchical display, an impediment not simply to the formation of self-government but to what he calls the "design" and "end" of government. That "design" and "end" are, exactly like "pattern" and "sway," the purposeful and structured means by which independence is exercised as a function of the law for Freneau and government for Paine.

Yet for Paine, the law serves its own deliberate ends, no less patterned than they are for Freneau: "Let a crown be placed thereon, by which the world will know, that so far as we approve of monarchy, that in America law is the king. For as in absolute governments the king is law, so in free countries the law ought to be king; and there ought to be no other. But lest any ill use should afterwards arise, let the crown at the conclusion of the ceremony be demolished, and scattered among the people whose right it is. A government of our own is our natural right."[5] Paine's view of law, while parallel to Freneau's, nonetheless engages in a different rhetorical and imaginative register. For Freneau, the law occupied the vacuum created by an eradicated crown, where it fills the space with pattern and presumably the darkness of dazzle's end with more persistent light. For Paine, dazzle is an effect more than a characteristic of the crown, preventing and impeding the very will to self-government. The law in Paine does not occupy a vacuum but replaces a king, a switch and not a novelty. The simple inversion is key for Paine; the law is not about the power vacuum necessitated by revolution, an idea rarely mentioned by either Freneau or Paine, but the natural consequence of what they are arguing. Paine views the law as a living rebuke to the king when the law, which had made him king, is now king itself.

That chiasmus is exactly how the "world will know" the value and excellence of the law. However, Paine's pamphlet is more attuned to the realities of political authority than Freneau's poem, and he insists that the crown worn by King Law "be demolished and scattered among the people whose right it is." The twinned acts of demolishing and scattering are for Paine what vanishing and patterning are for Freneau, the cause and effect of replacing the primacy of a monarch with the equality of the laws. "Demolish" would become a frequent poetic invocation for Freneau, generally representing his delight in the destruction and certain end of things, but in Paine's *Common Sense* there is little delight, only duty. That duty is for those who stand under the crown of law to take possession of it and to act in accordance with such possession. As such, "demolish" in Paine has little of ontological diminishment in it. To demolish is to destroy, but not completely; it is to keep fragments and debris that stand as testaments to what once stood. As well, if Freneau had imagined the law extending globally and becoming a pattern for the world, with its only, but crucial, American quality being "here" and "first," then for Paine, it is not that America broadcasts her laws around the world. Indeed, he acknowledges that other "free countries" already have similar legal practices. Instead, he sees that law must spread, individually and autonomously, in a society, socially before globally, and not as pattern but in pieces, with each person a subject to the law but no less an author of it.

Their shared visions and hope for American independence make Freneau's poetry and Paine's early prose easily allied, but as Freneau continued writing poetry after the American Revolution, he began to view Paine specifically as a figure who embodied in his writings, and his temperament, the best of what the progressive politics and fiery revolutions of the 1790s could achieve. If Paine was a powerful, spectral figure in 1790s English poetry, then in Freneau he is no less essential but more broadly employed and tangible. The reasons why reflect how Freneau understood the purpose and role of his own political poetry and prose in an era he largely devoted to newspaper editing. To some extent, this new literary, social, and media role allowed Freneau both the medium and the means to explore and write his Paine-focused poetry, as Paine was often in the very news Freneau was reporting. In terms of authorship, however, it is instructive to look at an early Freneau poem that contends with the conditions of contemporary authorship. "To An Author" was printed in the 1788 edition of Freneau's 1786 collected works. In it, he laments the lack of genius in critics, the increasingly crowded marketplace of ideas and books, and the fact that "An age employed in edging steel / Can no poetic raptures feel" (35–36). As a result,

On one, we fear, your choice must fall—
The least engaging of them all—
Her visage stern—an angry style—
A clouded brow—malicious smile—
A mind on murdered victims place—
She, only she, can please the taste! (44–49)

The author, here specifically the poet, cowers in front of the political and social upheavals of the last decade of the eighteenth-century, making it unrecognizable to the imagined first half, in part because Freneau was already starting to realize "the formal inadequacies of poetry representing the swirls and upheavals of democratic passions."[6] The poet's duty is no longer to speak beauty from nature, but merely to catalogue grief and advocate for victims, in a kind of desperate ventriloquism.

And yet, just four years later, in the first issue of his *National Gazette*, Freneau includes on his last page "A Poetical Address to the People of the United States."[7] It begins

This age is so fertile of mighty events
That people complain, with some reason, no doubt,
Besides the time lost, and besides the expence,
With reading the papers they're fairly worn out;
The *past* is no longer an object of care,
The *present* consumes all the time they can spare. (1–6)

Freneau sketches a hectic, erratic modern eighteenth-century culture, where in the span of three years, the "age employed in edging steel" has become "fertile with mighty events" and the newspapers that relate those events are ubiquitous and overwhelming for the average citizen. There is however, for Freneau, an ethic of reading, since it is the "best employment." That ethic justifies the existence of newspapers, and for Freneau especially, who often put his verse in newspapers, it motivates the newspaper editor as author, ultimately justifying both because

From the spark that we kindled a flame has gone forth
To expand thro' the world and enlighten mankind:
With a code of new doctrines the universe rings,
And *Thomas* is preaching strange sermons to kings. (21–24)[8]

Although "To An Author" is about poetry and the poet and "A Poetical Address" about news and the newspaper, the defining difference between their visions of authorship is not generic but epochal. "A Poetical Address" is published at least a year prior to Paine's *The Age of Reason,* but for Freneau, the age, in 1791, was already Paine's to define. As he would in his 1809 "Stanzas on the Decease of Thomas Paine," Freneau alludes to their shared deism as one of Paine's major contributions to the democratic movement. Paine "preaches" to kings, and his "sermons" introduce and expound upon a new "code of doctrine" that has universal appeal. This is an interesting political cosmology that specifically links Paine's deism, and his near religious level of intensity, with his political and revolutionary activities. That is why the sermons are "strange"—not simply otherworldly, unfamiliar, and unwelcomed by all monarchs, but "exceptionally great."[9]

This essential role of Paine in Freneau's complete suite of authorial activities is especially reflected in the 1795 edition of Freneau's poems. The overwhelmingly dark tone of "To An Author," essentially a self-critique on the 1786 edition of his poems, reveals Freneau's uneasy and tenuous relationship to his poetical corpus, but the 1795 edition is very much a product close to Freneau's heart. As Richard Vitzthum describes it, the 1795 *Poems,* self-published in Monmouth, New Jersey, "was a volume evidently designed to be his vehicle of communication with future generations of readers. Containing only a handful of new poems, none of major significance, the volume reveals Freneau's wish at the time to establish an authoritative canon."[10] While I agree that this volume was Freneau's attempt at establishing his legacy, I also contend that Freneau saw that legacy as intertwined with Paine's. Many of the poems focus on Paine and the French Revolution and are of great significance to Freneau's conception of Paine and his role in ushering in an age of reason and democracy. This is revealed at two specific points in the volume, the first about three quarters of the way through, with the poems "To My Book," "To The Public," and "To A Republican, With Mr. Paine's Rights of Man" forming a poetical triumvirate that makes stark claims to Freneau's and Paine's shared beliefs.

"To My Book" is a rollicking poem, essentially the companion piece to "To An Author," but instead of seeking models in early eighteenth-century poetic figures and critics, Freneau recasts his poetry as serving a decidedly political end:

Seven years are now elaps'd, dear rambling volume,
Since, to all knavish wights a foe,
I sent you forth to vex and gall 'em,
Or drive them to the shades below:
With spirit, still, of DEMOCRATIC proof. (1–5)

An entrepreneurial microbrewer of democracy, Freneau brackets the poem with another allusion to his democratic credentials:

> This I can say, you've spread your wings afar,
> Hostile to garter, ribbon, crown, and star;
> Still on the people's, still on Freedom's side,
> With full determin'd aim, to baffle every claim
> Of well-born wights, that aim to mount and ride. (29–33)

The terminal and caesural rhymes of aim (twice) and claim, with those "aims" diametrically opposed, bracket Freneau's attempt to preempt criticism and cast his writings at the service of democracy and rights. His repetition of "still" highlights his posture toward the people and freedom, both silent immovable guardians of what revolutions had already won and incipient revolutionaries continuously affecting revolutionary change, a recasting of his poetry as always democratic in claim and revolutionary in aim.

"To The Public" is the next poem, simply his "Poetical Address to the People of the United States" retitled with one emendation: "Thomas preaching strange sermons" has become "Paine preaching strange sermons." With his democratic credentials established in "To My Book," "To The Public," with its exploration of the editor's role as news provider and author, becomes the previous poem's natural heir. However, the poem which follows "To The Public" explicitly links these ideas of authorship and the sociopolitical role of the author. "To A Republican, With Mr. Paine's Rights of Man" opens with one of the best examples of Freneau's poetics:

> Thus briefly sketch'd the sacred Rights of Man,
> How inconsistent with the Royal Plan!
> Which for itself exclusive honour craves,
> Where some are masters born, and millions slaves.
> With what contempt must every eye look down
> On that base, childish bauble call'd a crown,
> The gilded bait, that lures the crowd, to come,
> Bow down their necks, and meet a slavish doom;
> The source of half the miseries men endure,
> The quack that kills them, while it seems to cure. (1–10)

The lines turn not so much around their description of corrupt monarchy undone by Paine's argument for human rights, as they do clustered sounds and repetitions of *m, c,* and *b.* The *m* emerges first, between "man," "masters," and "millions," with the last word delaying the natural binary of master and slaves, instead emphasizing the scope of a monarch's reign and the scale of what Paine achieves in advocating for rights. "Miseries" a line later amplifies this, since misery is what masters make and where millions meet. That in turn is balanced by the *b* sound, which surfaces in the opening line with "born," but then crowds into the dismissive *b* sounds of the "base bauble" that is "call'd a crown." The clash of the loose, almost languid *b* sounds and the hard *c* sounds enacts the clash between master and slave, the democratic defense of rights and the monarchical abuse of them. The "base bauble" then becomes "bait" with an echo of the clashing hard *c* sounds of "the crowd" that "comes." "Crowd" is virtually identical to "crown," but that is exactly the uniformity and unanimity Freneau wants undone and Paine wants to see empower the crowd: it is no less than resistance to "dazzle." The final *b* sound is one of submission, "bow," soon giving way both to the near echo of "down" and "doom" as well as to the inverse of the hard *c* sounds, namely the soft *s* sounds of "slavish" and "source," which harkens back to "slaves," "masters," and "millions." These opening lines end with the re-evocation of the hard *c* sound in "quack" and "cure," and the futility of its offer of consolation.

This verbal scheme continues throughout the poem, but in the subsequent lines Freneau turns from a criticism of monarchies to an encomium on Paine and his writing:

> Rous'd by the Reason of his manly page,
> Once more shall Paine a listening world engage:
> From Reason's source, a bold reform he brings,
> In raising up mankind, he pulls down kings. (11–14)

Freneau's designation of Paine's work as "manly" evokes the public virtue so essential to America's rising glory but also to Freneau's other early poetry, where it has been suggested that "Freneau sexualized ships to make the American case against the British," using "sexuality and gender thematically to subvert Britain's naval superiority."[11] Naval poetry seemed to be a potent subject for such sexualized understandings, but Freneau's claim here is somewhat different. It is the French, specifically, and all monarchies generally, including England's, that are spoken of here, and their crimes, as demonstrated above, are not allegorically or literally sexual in any way. There does, however, seem to be one way of grasping Freneau's claim, by recognizing how in his earlier poetry he "exploits the ambiguous possibilities of the ships' androgynous 'parts' [and] highlights the feminine virginity of the American brig while emphasizing the rapacious masculinity of the British frigate."[12] The sexual binary of male/female, and the possibility of androgyny, suggests that Freneau played with somewhat fluid definitions of gender in his naval poetry, and here it is not simply the singularly emphasized strength, energy, logic, and inevitable truthfulness of Paine's page that marks it as masculine, but also a treacherous, not victimized, woman:

> Now driven to wars, and now oppres'd at home,
> Compell'd in crowds o'er distant seas to roam,
> From India's climes the plundered prize to bring
> To glad the strumpet, or to glut the king. (31–34)

That "strumpet," while not exactly oppositional to Paine's "manly page," suggests exactly how masculine Paine's writings are. When they are "read and scann'd," those readers of *Rights of Man* "glow, at every line, with kindling rage" (26) and are "rous'd" to both defend their rights and press for political change. Paine's manliness begets a legitimized emotional response: deep, abiding anger. Monarchies are not feminized but often abuse power for feminine benefit, and it is only oppression and compulsion that make any subject serve their king and not their rights. The corresponding emotion is a sharp Freneau alliteration: glut and gladness. The king is bloated and full, the strumpet gladdened and satiated. If monarchies do justify their acts to satiate illicit sexual pleasures, then manliness corresponds and answers with an absent but gestured at rhyme for "glad": "mad."[13]

Paine's writing here is powerfully rendered, not so much as an intellectual triumph but a stick that pokes one into unheralded fury. And such fury is not merely the gendered affect of Paine's words. Instead, what Paine's manliness manifests itself against is clear from the interrelated nexus of terms that devolve out of the "Royal Plan" (2), which tasks kings,

> a dull designing few,
> To shackle beings that they scarcely knew,
> Who made this globe the residence of slaves,
> And built their thrones on systems form'd by knaves. (19–22)

"Plan," "design" and "system" all have the related qualities of exacting preparedness, full intention, and completion of vision that implies a certain rigidity of both thought and action tending toward a tyrannical goal. It is cold and exacting, the antithesis of the spark of passion that Paine provokes. This is method, the opposite of passion that is "rous'd" and "kindled." Paine's persuasive prose defense for the rights of man disquiets such rigidity and certitude by moving in great bouts of energy from author to reader and page to mind. Such responses are unique in themselves, as unique as each act of "scanning" is to a text, while the systems of monarchy are automatic, fueled by compulsion and oppression. That lock-step near automation allows Freneau to show the human cost of such monarchical posturing, since kings make slaves of those they "hardly know." System is an essential kingly dehumanization of their subjects; Paine's *Rights of Man* is the rehumanization of the crowd through their individual acts of reading.

If, however, Paine's *Rights of Man* is ideal tinder for such arousal, Freneau also wants to suggest the need for a larger, national effort under which such readings could fruitfully demolish monarchy. The solution for Freneau in this poem is the figure of Columba. A number of Freneau's poems from the 1790s and in the 1795 edition end in an address to Columba, Freneau's shorthand for America after the revolution. As he claims in the final lines of the poem:

> Columba, hail! immortal be thy reign:
> Without a king, we till the smiling plain;
> Without a king, we trace the unbounded sea,
> And traffic round the globe, through each degree;
> . . . .
> Without a king, the Laws maintain their sway,
> While honour bids each generous heart obey. (35–38, 41–42)

The "sway" of law returns from "The Rising Glory of America," here not so much rising as settled as part of the great republic, and its rhyme, "obey," perfectly reflects the conditions under which the law maintains its sway, namely willed duty to its exercise. "Without a king" rings like the great American chorus, and the actions of the great "we," which both personalizes and unites individual acts of reading, here are those which counteract and contest the royal plan, namely "tilling" and the "tracing" of the "unbounded sea." This very much reflects Freneau's frequent land/sea dichotomy, but instead of "the sea . . . connot[ing] to Freneau the destructive, chaotic, inhuman aspects of nature," and the land representing "benevolent, harmonious, and passive aspects of nature," those diametrically opposed notions of land and sea are now merged into one, because the acts of controlling them, namely "tilling" and "tracing," are in the poem linked directly to the emotional fervor that Paine arouses.[14] As well, since in Freneau's earlier readings land and sea were also gendered, with sea being masculine and land feminine, this line suggests that Paine's manly page has united those two aspects and made it so there is no easy dichotomy of male and female, land and sea, but only that which sits under the influence of Paine's text. Those rights are universal, and such universality means that gendered distinctions disappear into Columba's "guardianship" of the rights for which Paine's text argues.

With this necessary addition to Freneau's already zealous commitment to America and its guardianship of the rights of man, there remains only the means to sustain it:

> So shall our nation, form'd on Virtue's plan,
> Remain the guardian of the Rights of Man,
> A vast Republic, fam'd through every clime,
> Without a king, to see the end of time. (47–50)

A "plan" now belongs to virtue, not royalty, if only because it belongs to the very manliness that Paine exudes from his text; the ends and the execution are radically, essentially different, and are so because in opposition to the idea of a royal system that is self-enclosed and regulated strictly, the final stanza banks America's guardianship of the rights of man on the same qualities as the unbounded sea: its "vastness." It is the immensity of America, understood as both a geographical expansiveness and the space where the rights of man could flourish. It is also fundamentally temporal; America will remain "without a king" in order to "see the end of time," inculcating the linear distance of near eternity (or at least an unknown end) with America's sempiternal guardianship of human rights. Since they too are boundless, then the only possible nation that could defend them needs by necessity to be as universal as those very rights are for Paine. And so for Freneau, they could only be ascribed to a nation as expansive, and thus desystematized, as "Columba."

And with that proleptic, quasiprophetic end to "To A Republican, With Mr. Paine's Rights of Man," the three poems from the near end of Freneau's 1795 edition form an assertive group claim to Freneau's emerging understanding of his authorship but also of Paine's heroism: his essential role in what America had become in the years after the revolution, and what he contributes to the global rejection of monarchy and embrace of democracy. It is not America, though, that draws Freneau's attention as the volume draws to a close. Instead, it is the country in which much of the revolutionary activity of the 1790s had occurred: France, in the poem "On the Demolition of the French Monarchy." Celebrating the downfall of Louis XVII and his queen, Freneau combines the images of freedom and the liberty tree: "In

Virtue's cause, I see unite / Worlds, under Freedom's Tree!" (38–39). What
follows virtue is its companion, "valor":

> Valor, at length, by Fortune led,
> The Rights of Man restores;
> And Gallia, now from bondage freed,
> Her rising sun adores:
> On Equal Rights, her fabric plann'd,
> Storms idly round it rave,
> No longer breathes in Gallic land
> A monarch, or a slave! (40–47)

The collapse of those two social categories, monarch and slave, not into a
single category but into nonexistent categories, is the catalyst behind the
"restoration" of the rights of man, exposing those social titles as arbitrary
and false and, as such, the rights of man as natural. As Paine says in *Rights
of Man:* "Natural rights are those which appertain to man in right of his
existence. . . . Civil rights are those which appertain to man in right of
his being a member of society. Every civil right has for its foundation some
natural right pre-existing in the individual."[15] By "restoring" the rights of
man, the French Revolution does not simply revert man to his natural
rights, it collapses artificial social categories in order to make possible the
sociopolitical conditions for these very exchanges of civil and natural rights,
and the power distribution that allows for the making of distinctions between one's individual rights and one's civil rights. It is then in the eradication of distinctions that equality arises, along with the rights both held and
exchanged that secure that equality. This is the very "fabric" of France and of
what the "world, under the Freedom Tree," both needs and demands. "Plan"
here reappears, cleansed from its obsessive automation and links to tyrannical, monarchical policy toward the monarch's subjects. What the "plan"
of equal rights effects is the enduring place of a heroic Paine in the
history of the dissemination of equal rights. Likewise, it strengthens
the inextricably linked devotion of France, the world, and Paine to the
"Democratic Cause":

> O France! The world to thee must owe
> A debt they ne'er can pay:
> The Rights of Man you bid them know,
> And kindle Reason's day! (103–7)

Freneau seems to have poetically rendered what Paine himself says not in *Rights of Man* but *The Age of Reason:* "There are two distinct classes of what are called thoughts—those that we produce in ourselves by reflection and the act of thinking, and those that bolt into the mind of their own accord."[16] Freneau's "know" encompasses both of those senses—something that appeals, upon further reflection, to an innate, natural sense of right, but that also "bolts" into the mind as reason's kindling. That such knowledge is the very "debt" the world "owes" to France, but can never pay, means that France is the very model and, yes, pattern of the distribution and protection of equal rights both individually and civilly expressed, by which reason's new day is measured.

By the end of the 1795 volume, Freneau and Paine are together on the cusp of a new world and the establishment of reason's day as the new age in which politics is irrevocably changed, democracy spread around the globe, equal rights protected by those emergent democracies, and Paine heroically celebrated as the pillar of "truth . . . vouchsaf'd to learn" (62), the very spark kindling the emergence of epochal renewal. That optimism in Paine and his politics maintained its strength in Freneau from 1795 until 1809, when Paine died. In a letter to his friend Dr. John Francis in 1815, Freneau mentions some of the poetry he was about to publish anew. After discussing the bibliographic details of the new edition, he goes on to say, "Others smell out deism in the Book because it contains a few stanzas, insignificant examples, to the Memory of poor Thomas Paine."[17] That poem is "Stanzas on the Decease of Thomas Paine," and Freneau's complaint that his volume would "smell" of deism because of this poem reflects its clever use of deistic principles to frame Paine's death through his deconstruction of organized religion in *The Age of Reason.*

> Princes and kings decay and die
> And instant, rise again:
> But this is not the case, trust me
> With men like Thomas Paine.
>
> In vain the democratic host
> His equal would attain:
> For years to come they will not boast
> A second Thomas Paine.
>
> Though many may his name assume;
> Assumption is in vain;

For every man has not his plume—
Whose name is Thomas Paine. (1–12)

The cascade of religious terms is ironic in opposition: the phrases "rise again," "host," and "assumption" all have religious connotations, but within the poem have purely secular denotations serving to highlight Paine's rejection of institutionalized religion and the utter falsity of proclaimed miracles like heavenly assumptions. As Paine himself writes, "Since, then, no external evidence can, at this long distance of time, be produced to prove whether the Church fabricated the doctrine called redemption or not . . . the case can only be referred to the internal evidence which the thing carries of itself; and this affords a very strong presumption of its being a fabrication."[18] Paine's own sense of fabrication is of course not Freneau's, yet Paine's absolute insistence on external and internal synchronicity as the benchmark for religious truth finds its way into Freneau's poem:

To tyrants and the tyrant crew,
Indeed, he was the bane;
He writ, and gave them all their due,
And signed it,—Thomas Paine. (17–20)

Whether as "man" or as a "signature," Paine, even in death, is consistent, a bulwark against both Christian critics and those who sought to undermine his politics. His singularity as someone who cannot be redeemed, or resurrected, is the mark of his only "redemption," and that which makes him simply a part of the nature in which any deist sees the only testament to God's existence.

However, such a failure to return, or the leaving of Paine's reputation in the hands of those who merely want him back, would ultimately signify victory for Paine's opponents, and for Freneau the solution is an easy one:

Oh! how we loved to see him write
And curb the race of Cain!
They hope and wish that Thomas P——
May never rise again.

What idle hopes!—yes—such a man
May yet appear again.—
When they are dead, they die for aye:
Not so with Thomas Paine. (21–28)

The two stanzas mark very noticeable shifts in the poem. In the first, Paine, who usually occupies the last line of each stanza, is moved to the penultimate line. This acts as a very clear signifier that the tone and argument of the poem is about to shift, from celebrating Paine's uniqueness to worrying about it. His enemies wish he may never rise again, but those are merely "idle hopes." Palpable anxiety dwells in the frequent use of dashes but is swallowed up by the anticlimactic conviction of the final lines. Freneau is hesitant in the first two lines of the stanza, but the finality of death, contrasted to the assumptive opening, responds. When Paine's enemies are dead, they are dead—gone to the world but also validating, perhaps even proving, Paine's own views of the afterlife, or at least his criticisms of the Judeo-Christian concept of it. Paine, though, simply does not die: "not so Thomas Paine." Paine will live and thrive through his writings, but that seems too easy. There is, in the end, no real answer there, just an affirmation of a negative, and a sense that Paine, in his writings, in his influence, and in his sheer force of personality, may have guaranteed or won what his enemies could not: a legacy. Such was his heroism. It is a legacy and a heroism Freneau himself helped to grow through his poetry, even, it seems, or especially, at the cost of his own.

EIGHT

Repay Thy Labors

Joel Barlow's Poetic Predilections

But Thomas Paine, as a visiting acquaintance and as a literary friend, the only points of view from which I knew him, was one of the most instructive men I have ever known.

—Joel Barlow, *Letter on the Life of Thomas Paine*

In Harvard's Houghton Library rests Joel Barlow's manuscript plan for his own *Collected Works*.[1] Near the bottom, the eleventh of fifteen items comprising his proposed second volume, lies a piece that has never actually been published in any edition of Barlow's works: *Letter on the Life of Thomas Paine*.[2] Having written it in response to a request from James Cheetham, erstwhile biographer of Paine, Barlow initially requested that the letter not be printed. Cheetham promptly ignored Barlow's entreaty and included parts of it in his biography.[3] The letter is an evenhanded, somewhat nostalgic and regretful piece, which calls Paine "one of the most benevolent and disinterested of mankind, endowed with the clearest perception, an uncommon share of original genius, and the greatest breadth of thought," and concludes with the epigraph above. Although their shared political views are evident in works like Barlow's *Advice to the Privileged Orders* (1792), I would contend that the degree to which Paine was an instructive literary friend to Barlow is best measured by Paine's deep influence on Barlow's major literary works *The Vision of Columbus* and *The Columbiad*. To the former, Paine's *A Letter Addressed to the Abbé Raynal* acts as an imaginative framework for Barlow's cosmopolitan exploration of government and its osmotic limits; to the latter, Paine's arguments about the nature and extent of system as a concept and consequence of revolution demarcates Barlow's own cosmopolitan theory of rights, the generic contentions of his American epic, and, ultimately, his shared literary destiny with Paine, the "visiting acquaintance."

The Vision of Columbus was first published in 1787, with Paine listed as one of the poem's subscribers. Opening with an angel showing the despondent, imprisoned Columbus a vision of the Americas and its first peoples, Barlow describes both in terms deliberately reminiscent of Paine's in *Common Sense:*

> A scanty band
> In that far age, approach'd the untrodden land.
> Prolific wilds, with game and fruitage crown'd,
> Supply'd their wishes from the uncultured ground.
> By nature form'd to rove, the restless mind,
> Of freedom fond, will ramble unconfined,
> Till all the realm is fill'd, and rival right
> Restrains their steps, and bids their force unite;
> When common safety builds a common cause,
> Conforms their interests and inspires their laws;
> By mutual checks their different manners blend,
> Their fields bloom joyous and their walls ascend.
>
> Here, to their growing hosts, no bounds arose,
> They claim'd no safeguard, as they fear'd no foes. (2:245–56)

The "uncultured" land, frequently invoked by Barlow, would find an echo in Paine's later *Agrarian Justice,* and here in the poem its effortless offering of all basic resources for a nascent society echoes Paine's own view on how societies develop and acquire the need for government: "Let us suppose a small number of persons settled in some sequestered part of the earth, unconnected with the rest. . . . It will unavoidably happen that in proportion as they surmount the first difficulties of emigration, which bound them together in a common cause, they will begin to relax in their duty and attachment to each other: and this remissness will point out the necessity of establishing some form of government to supply the defect of moral virtue."[4] Barlow's poetic imagining of Mesoamerica's prehistoric beginnings and Paine's classical formulation of the "design and end" of government share many of the same ideological impulses save for an essential and deferred distinction. This habit of sharing a general political and ideological framework but working it to different ends perfectly characterizes Barlow's management of Paine's influence on his poetic texts. Both incipient visions here contend that the isolated and pristine natures, both human and geographical, of indigenous groups affords them a natural liberty or "fond freedom." Through Paine's mutual need, the bonds of society are built; for Barlow "mutual checks" restrain and thus cohere native differences into a socially constructive whole. For Barlow, "common safety builds a common cause" because such safety is found in check, while for Paine "common cause" is a "reciprocal blessing."[5] Paine's necessity, the "gravitating power," takes in Barlow the form of the "restless mind" that propels forward the conforming of interest and inspiration into laws. This insistence upon "mindfulness" as a socially progressive necessity would come to be an indispensable component of Barlow's poetic view of sociability and its centrality to his vision. That vision parallels Paine's own, yet while Paine's account ultimately becomes a progressive fable of humanity's lack of moral virtue and perfect justice, Barlow makes no such claim about human nature, nor ultimately about the absolute need and inevitable path to government as a consequence of mutual check.[6] Instead, the culmination of the passage rests in the phrase "no bounds arose." The imaginative tension between the "walls ascending"— a boundary of urban development and progress, of the first inclination toward civilization, and decidedly not for "safeguarding" against "foes"—and their boundless restraint under "rival right," presents an image of a people who form society's basic infrastructure due not to failed human nature but to the transformation of a restrictive, necessary restraint ("mutual check") into a positive social connection ("manners blend") by shifting internal mechanisms of self-control into external institutions of assertive stability.

This equilibrium between the internal cultivation of self-control and the establishment of institutional norms that socially enforce it is rendered in the poem in a favorite and deliberate Barlow shorthand, "social love," although there are several permutations of such "social" values in the poem.[7] The term is borrowed deliberately from James Thomson, whose own use of "heaven-directed social love . . . has always inspired patriots and true heroes," but in Barlow such social love is more horizontal than vertical, generated inter alia amongst members of a progressing society, heaven-on-earth creating more than simply directed.[8] As such, I would suggest that Barlow's notion of social love owes something to Paine's "Boston" passage in the third part of *Common Sense*, where a calculated cultivation of transnational sympathy had impelled Paine's readers to create the very notion of nation. Self-love for Paine is in the national interest; in Barlow it is the national cause. In addition, if I have pointed to imagination as a critical interpretive tool for Paine's leveraging of national sympathy, it should likewise be noted that for Barlow, social love in all its permutations depends upon a cultivated mindfulness—self-perception that bleeds into institutional growth and its attendant control mechanisms while affirming both their necessity and need—which constitutes the basic building block of the nation state and the move from primitive tribalism to nation.

It is then Thomson, the major paratextual influence on *Common Sense*, who serves as an important conduit between Paine and Barlow.[9] In *The Vision of Columbus*, through Paine's own use of Thomson in *Common Sense*, Barlow's calculated poetic adoption of social love serves as the connective tissue between individual action and historical institutional development that ultimately propels his vision forward toward its progressive end. In aggregate, this constellation of "social" virtues predicated upon a foundational love points to Barlow's view that it is in the abandonment of all violent and belligerent tendencies, and an orientation beyond nationalistic formations, that the social, intimate connections that forge societies are not merely formed but perfected:

> Now, borne on bolder wings, with happier flight,
> The world's broad bounds unfolding to the sight,
> The mind shall soar; the nations catch the flame,
> Enlarge their counsels and extend their fame;
> While mutual ties the social joys enhance,
> And the last stage of civil rule advance. (2:425–30)

Through "mutual tie" and "social joy," that "last stage of civil rule" is the perfectible apex of the societal dependence on human and institutional methods of control; that same dynamism of mutual ties and social joys is crucially for Barlow the very actions that make the mind "soar" and generate a kind of transcendent mind reifying the commitment and exercise of societal bonds into a complete, terminal whole that can counteract "the horror of . . . moral hollowness, men and women emptied of will and ethical purpose and moving mindlessly about the social stage as mere passive creatures."[10] Social joy is a hedge against such passivity; one cannot help but be socially active and exercise social agency when what joy and agency share is identical. "Enlarge" suggests the sense of "to widen, render more comprehensive (a person's thoughts, sympathies, affections)," while "extend" suggests spatial and temporal extension as well as the legal sense of "to seize upon (land, etc.) in satisfaction for a debt." These senses deepen the social commitment demanded by Barlow in order to mindfully reach the "last stage," because they fully engage the qualities of mechanisms both human and institutional, poetic shorthand for the processes in action and perfected here.[11] Barlow's vision depends heavily on this deliberately fashioned mindfulness and affective equilibrium. By fostering and developing minds deeply entrenched in civic concern, and in turn constructing within society the supports for growing those minds, which in turn strengthens the bonds of society, every and each of those social constellations are confirmed. The synchronicity between the internal cultivation of social love and the external, constructed infrastructure of those bonds creates the perfectibility of all social virtues.

While the rest of the poem courses through North American history as a consequence of soaring mindfulness cultivated by social virtues, the fulfillment of the vision and the greatest extension of the social virtues' mental configurations rests in book 9. What Barlow offers as the natural progression of his constellation of social values reaches its peak in a loosely cosmopolitan post-revolutionary world:

> [Columbus] saw the nations tread their different shores,
> Ply their own toils and claim their local powers.
> He mark'd what tribes still rove the savage waste,
> What happier realms the sweets of plenty taste. (9:23–26)

The distinct proprietary individualism of each nation, which in the angel's vision includes both enlightened and "savage" nations, serves as a kind of placeholder, since the angel "extends" Columbus's vision out into a progressive future:

> See, thro' the whole, the same progressive plan,
> That draws, for mutual succor, man to man,
> From friends to tribes, from tribes to realms ascend,
> Their powers, their interests, and their passions blend;
> Adorn their manners, social virtues spread,
> Enlarge their compacts, and extend their trade. (9:45–50)

In imagining the growth of "local powers" to a globally progressive plan "through the whole," Barlow poetically renders a cosmopolitan vision out of which finally emerges a comprehensive social virtue expanding beyond the merely personal and institutional to the global. "Mutual succor" here both activates the previously passive "mutual ties" and echoes Paine's own impetus to societal formation, but for Barlow the "ascent" generated by that "succor" is progressively broader—from friends to tribes to realms—as much as vertical, and given the sense of ascent as "to rise by growth or construction," it is the deliberate result of the mindfulness he exhorts from his readers.[12] No longer passive players on the social stage, they are thus activated and empowered agents of the new globalism's ascent. The echoed hard *c* of "counsel" and "compacts," and the assonantal near-rhyme of "fame" and "trade," link Barlow's poetic movement from mindfulness and perfectible social virtues to what amounts to a cultivated and enlighteningly self-aware global consciousness whose agents create their own environment for practicing those virtues through mutual, and here economic, accord. The outward expansion of the individual relationship to one that induces the formation of nations and the generation of a global network characterized by friendship between those nations is both perpetuated and guaranteed by the tripartite actionability of what the angel reveals to Barlow, namely the affective states that accompany and parallel these global networks.

Like "manners" in the first instance of society, these states "blend." While it is manners, a kind of shorthand for social action in a global economy, or global consciousness rendered affectively, that are "adorned" and thus naturally embellished, the three distinctly enlarging metaphors of growth and increase, "spread," "enlarge," and "extend," poetically pitch Barlow's vision as both inevitable and engrossing, really vertical and horizontal for the first and only time in the poem. Although the social virtues spread, and thus come "fully to the mind and eye" as a kind of self-fulfilling virtue, the ideological linking of "spread" as an action similar if not identical to both enlarging in its comprehension and extending in its sense of "taking possession of fully" means that a clear and necessary shift has occurred, from mere mindfulness to "manners," and from the mind that soars to the virtues that spread. As the mind becomes more important as a divine attribute than a human faculty in the final book ("Enough for thee, that thy delighted mind / Should trace the deeds and blessings of thy kind," 9:259–60), it must be considered why the absence of mind here is a calculated gambit on Barlow's part and a necessary sacrifice at the altar of progress.

This calculated abandonment of the mind as a necessary but not necessarily deleterious effect of the "accordant whole" is, I would suggest, certainly influenced by Paine's *A Letter Addressed to the Abbé Raynal.* That letter contains the first and most thorough expression of Paine's cosmopolitan vision:

> The principal and almost only remaining enemy . . . is *prejudice;* for it is evidently the interest of mankind to agree and make the best of life. . . .

There is now left scarcely anything to quarrel about, but what arises from that demon of society, prejudice, and the consequent sullenness and intractableness of the temper.

There is something exceedingly curious in the constitution and operation of prejudice. It has the singular ability of accommodating itself to all the possible varieties of the human mind.[13]

Paine's view of prejudice as an instinctive barrier to progress remains as strong in the *Letter* as it was in *Common Sense.* Here, he articulates prejudice's deleterious staying power, its persistent capacity to remain in the mind despite the positive effects of science, education, and globalization, which Barlow too sees as enlightening the human mind. That difference, namely the ability of enlightenment knowledge to eradicate prejudice, is key to how Paine and Barlow together see the operations of globalism on the human mind and manners. They do so in a chiasmatic reversal of the lines in book 4 in which *Common Sense* is invoked, as the fulfillment of a previously noted poetic deferral. For Barlow, it is only in "accordant union" and the move beyond local powers that the "cares of state," namely government, become important:

> While thus the realms their mutual glories lend,
> Unnumber'd fires the cares of state attend;
> Blest with each human art, and skill'd to find,
> Each wild device that prompts the wayward mind;
> What soft restraints the untemper'd breast requires,
> To taste new joys and cherish new desires. (9:167–72)

What Paine saw as the impelled conclusion to social conditions and the political arising out of the social, Barlow imagines as one of the many boundaries within which social virtue in a truly global world operates, while simultaneously situating government as the very boundary that must be persistently transgressed in order to assure the progress that defines "spreading," "enlarging," and "extending" as expansive states of the global network. For Paine government is a negative limit, for Barlow a positive limit to transgress in service to progressive history.[14] Government and the cares of state become important only in a global community impelling and urging those governments to think beyond their mere local powers, their authority ratified by their participation in cosmopolitan relations.

Within Barlow's poetic imagination, the operations of such progress and its attendant social virtues must be ones of egress and transgress, boundaries established and broken, yet for Paine in the *Letter*, the relationship between the temperable mind and an emergent, enlightened globalism is not a matter of boundaries and limits but of proportion and scale:

> The circle of civilization is yet incomplete. Mutual wants have formed the individuals of each country into a kind of national society, and here the progress of civilization has stopped. For it is easy to see, that nations with regard to each other (notwithstanding the ideal civil law, which every one explains as it suits him) are like individuals in a state of nature. They are regulated by no fixed principle, governed by no compulsive law, and each does independently what it pleases or what it can.
>
> Were it possible we could have known the world when in a state of barbarism, we might have concluded that it never could be brought into the order we now see it. The untamed mind was then as hard, if not harder, to work upon in its individual state, than the national mind is in its present one. Yet we have seen the accomplishment of one, why then should we doubt that of the other?[15]

Here is a scaled, geo-metric intentionally made for Paine's vision of a new world order. Just as they are for the individual, the same ideas and frameworks must be applied on a national scale. There are only nations for Paine, and just as individuals cohered into societies under governments due to their mutual wants and needs, so inherently do nations. The key for Paine is the fact that no different from the individual, the nation itself has a "mind" by which its actions and operations can be judged and assessed for its compatibility with the new global union. Tamed only in the tumult of the democratic revolution that had swept America and from there the world, the very notion of a national, "democratic" mind, more so than blended manners, becomes for Paine a cohesive unity—a real, palpable *e pluribus unum* that has a natural affinity for the new global reality because it has been trained through revolutionary discourse to think exclusively in global terms.[16]

For Barlow, who has rendered the mind as the preeminent boundary to be built and transcended, that same affinity takes a different tack:

> No more the noble patriotic mind,
> To narrow views and local laws confined,
> 'Gainst neighbouring lands directs the public rage,
> Plods for a realm or counsels for an age;

But lifts a larger thought, and reaches far,
Beyond the power, beyond the wish of war;
For realms and ages forms the general aim,
Makes patriot views and moral views the same. (9:193–200)

This then is global—hypersocial—love, and in the action of making patriot (transnational) and moral (personal) views the same, Barlow collapses the space Paine leaves for the operations of prejudice. Indeed, Barlow's debt to Paine is not just a view about the inevitably progressive and global union that the revolution created, nor is it really an incisive articulation of the ideological ends of cosmopolitanism, although there lies great sympathy between Paine and Barlow in those areas. Rather, it is his insistence on the centrality of the "democratic" mind, with its "initial plasticity but (potential) subsequent fixity" that Paine gives to Barlow as the essential element in his own global vision.[17] Ultimately shifted from human faculty to divine attribute, that mind in Barlow is the essential boundary not so much plastic or fixed but meant to measure how much the manners and social virtues move beyond it as the definitive codes of the new global order. And when those manners and virtues reach beyond measure, the product is a global consciousness, bolstered by a universal language, that answers in the visionary affirmative Paine's question. Having seen the accomplishment of one, you cannot doubt the other.[18]

However, such accomplishments did not follow from *The Vision*, and in 1807 Barlow reworked the poem into *The Columbiad.* Previous accounts of the changes between poems have generally tended to rest on the poem's genre. It was the shifting if not radical redefinition of the epic poem that motivated Barlow to make necessary emendations between editions, as Barlow came to see the epic as fulfilling "a tradition founded, not only upon change, but upon conscious reshaping of its own defining qualities."[19] Yet I would suggest that given the connections of *The Vision* to *Common Sense*, and through *Common Sense* to James Thomson, the poem, despite its open pretensions to being an epic, is best read as a kind of progress poem. Indeed, given its lush descriptions of North American geography and idealistic emphasis on education as an instrument of enlightenment, Barlow's progress poem is centered on what critics like R. H. Griffith consider the two essential *translatios,* or thematic considerations and transformations, necessary for progress poems to operate as publicly and culturally critical works of literature, namely empire and the arts.[20] It is by considering *The Columbiad* and *The Vision* as progress poems, not as epics, that we can see "the important change between the two versions," described by William Dowling as lying "not in the scattered doctrinal interpolations that are indeed to be encountered in the body and notes of *The Columbiad* but in its far greater power of demystification, its ability to gaze steadfastly through the illusory appearances thrown up by ideology."[21] And given Barlow's claims in the preface to *The Columbiad* that the poem's purpose was to "inculcate the love of rational liberty, and to discountenance the deleterious passion for violence and war," the reworking of *The Vision of Columbus* into *The Columbiad* highlights the ideological workings of the progress poem by drawing upon Paine's pointed ambivalence regarding one particular act as the barometer of success for those very *translatios*, "beyond the known limits of classical republicanism and covenant theology into unchartered ideological waters": the foment and action of war.[22] It is no less than war that becomes the main agent of "demystification" in the poem, an understanding of which Barlow inherits directly from Paine.[23]

In *The Vision*, war is terrible but also terribly necessary. Barlow's claims in that poem for the constellation of social virtues are often presented in relation to warfare, and its necessity is in part rooted in its opposition to the spreading of global virtue:

> Even horrid war, that erst her course withstood,
> And whelm'd, so oft, her peaceful shrines in blood,
> Now leads thro' paths unseen her glorious way,
> Extends her limits and confirms her sway. (8:137–40)

War drenches the temples of peace in blood but also "extends limits" and "confirms sway," a shrewd and fortuitous combination of individual heroism and governmental policy that together disseminate and contain the values that emerged victorious at the end of the revolution and likewise broaden the motions of globalism's reach. Barlow later in the poem suggests that "no rude war, that sweeps the crimson plain,/ Shall dare disturb the labours of the main" (9:75–76), yet in *The Vision*'s idealistic presentation of the world as a confederacy of nations and peoples, war becomes the necessary precondition for such a confederacy and that which is ultimately not banished but held in reserve as a pernicious vestige of the prejudiced mind.

One could turn to Paine's 1787 tract *Prospects on the Rubicon* for his views on war contemporaneous to the publication of *The Vision*, but it is the first part of *Rights of Man* that lays the full groundwork for Paine's political theory of war. There, Paine enumerates three conditions for war to happen: the right of declaring it, the ability to fund it, and the capacity to conduct it.[24] He collapses the first two while highlighting France's policy: putting the right where the expense is, by having the people, meaning the nation, and not the government both declare war and hold the purse strings for its conduct. That paradigmatic shift in who declares and funds war is taken up again in the work's concluding section. He repeats his arguments for war as a means of increasing revenue, but this time adds that "in any event of war, in the manner they are now commenced and concluded, the power and interests of governments are increased."[25] This last point makes legitimate war a rare reality in Paine's view. There is something essentially exponential about war; it increases beyond measure both the financial obligation and the very structures of governments who wage it. Given his inclination toward the scaled metrics of globalism, it must be seen that war's inevitable "exponential" growth is Paine's strongest argument against the very possibility of waging a legitimate war. Consequently, "War, therefore from its productiveness, as it easily furnishes the pretense of necessity for taxes and appointments to places and offices, becomes a principle part of the system of old governments. . . . The frivolous matters upon which war is made, show the disposition and avidity of governments to uphold the system of war, and betray the motives on which they act."[26] These thoughts on war have been called "a commitment . . . to modern democratic peace theory," but the real incisiveness of the passage comes from the use of system, wielded like a verbal cudgel against the horror not simply of profitable war but of incessant government expansion.[27] More than a mere mechanism of government, war becomes for Paine a natural part of it. Taking up the imagery of exponential growth, the key is that war is not fought on principle or for any purpose other than its own repetition; it is rather "productive," like a kind of manufacturing, and meant to increase itself at all costs. In that it is nothing other than a system. In fact, Paine suggests two modes of system here. War is a system itself, but it is a system that merges with another system, namely "old governments." This is a symptom of war as a natural part of those very "old governments." Indeed, systems are typically closed and ultimately automated, an ideal metaphor for the hereditary structures of power that propagate wars, and what underlies Paine's argument here is the essential functionality of systems, namely the feedback loop. Of the feedback loop as technical, philosophical, and political principle, Kevin Kelly writes: "The consequence of this automatic control (resulting from the feedback loop's minute and continuous self-corrections) is that the engineers could relax their ceaseless straining for perfectly uniform raw materials, perfectly regulated processes. Now they could begin with imperfect materials, imprecise processes. . . . Starting with the same quality of materials, the feedback loop could be set for a much higher quality setting, delivering increased precision for the next in line."[28] This argument for automation is Paine's for war. Both are cyclical actions by which initial imprecision leads directly to increased precision and much higher quality—for Paine, both in terms of the revenues that enrich and the lucrative branches that grow out of government. Indeed, each new war is an opportunity for minute "self-corrections" that propagate themselves in subsequent wars, and for which there is never need to worry about perfection since war corrects itself through those very offices that adhere to governments. But for Paine, likewise, the very product of war is war itself: a system that generates another system, and war a system and the product of another system, a perverse network theory that, like Barlow's view of war in *The Vision*, is the destructive, persistent remnant of prejudice.

That absolute insistence on war as system had a deep impact on Barlow's reimagining of violence and war in *The Columbiad*. This is not to say that "system" as a term is absent from *The Vision*, merely that its thematic use in *The Columbiad* is more essential to the poem's genre and its arguments about the deleterious effects of war and the nature of society. To some extent what the *translatios* progress toward in Barlow is the very notion of system. In *The Vision*, as Paine would do extensively in *The Age of Reason*, Barlow loosely renders system as an organized arrangement of celestial bodies, or a kind of celestial infrastructure for God's blessings upon society:

> Then blest religion leads the raptur'd mind
> Thro' brighter fields and pleasures more refin'd;
> Teaches the roving eye, at one broad view,
> To glance o'er time and look existence thro',
> See worlds, and worlds, to Being's formless end,
> With all their hosts, on one dread Power depend,
> Seraphs and suns and systems round him rise,
> Live in his life and kindle from his eyes. (9:317–24)

Later in book 9, Barlow presents "A sire elect" who

> Bid[s] one great empire, with extensive sway,
> Spread with the sun and bound the walks of day,
> One centered system, one all-ruling soul,
> Live thro' the parts, and regulate the whole. (435–38)

Whether here centered, and thus the administrative hub (or functional heart) of the blessed empire upon which the sun never sets, or one of three

listed celestial entities, system in Barlow's earlier poem is secondary and de-
rivative. Unrelated to war at all and subject to the admittedly broad limits of
a divinely benighted global empire, system is merely the effect of his vision.

The Columbiad radically repositions the poem in regards to war, and specifically in Paine's sense of war as system, which he further articulates in
Rights of Man:

> As war is the system of government on the old construction, the an-
> imosity which nations reciprocally entertain, is nothing more than
> what the policy of their governments excites, to keep up the spirit of
> the system. . . . Man is not the enemy of man, but through the me-
> dium of a false system of government. Instead therefore, of exclaim-
> ing against the ambition of kings, the exclamation should be directed
> against the principle of such governments; and instead of seeking to
> reform the individual, the wisdom of a nation should apply itself
> to reform the system.[29]

The passage turns on two consequences of system and war as system: spirit
and reform. The first is the function of system as the byproduct of automation. Closed off from its essential function, but likewise its very productivity,
all the outsider to system can do is maintain its spirit—its presumptive necessity and its benefit to the nation. Spirit fills the breach between perfect
and imperfect materials and processes. Of course, if spirit is the collective
acknowledgment of the perfectibility and necessity of system, then reform is
system's nodes. Systems have nodes, loci of those very self-corrections that
improve not the self but the system as a whole. System rationalizes only
other systems, system perfects only itself, and the nodes of correction, here
imagined as the individuals of a nation and not the government that runs it,
serve the system, not vice versa

The idea that systems have nodes that beget other systems merges seam-
lessly with Barlow's views on both society and war in *The Columbiad*. It may
well be a "monster" according to Barlow, but war is a system that inevitably
produces a cascade of related and essential systems, not surprisingly spurred
as nodal products of war and, in Barlow's peculiar poetical view, war's end.
Drawn toward "nobler aims" than conflict (10:263), Barlow's Bard "bids the
world" to "O'er cultured earth the rage of conquest cease,/War sink in night
and nature smile in peace" (10:265, 267–68). From this new perspective, the
Bard is able to

> behold
> New suns ascend and other skies unfold,
> Social and system'd worlds around him shine,
> And lift his living strains to harmony divine. (10:273–76)

Here, rather than one in a list of celestial bodies, or the consequences of divine imperialism, system is clearly coterminous with the social; the fact that worlds acquire a social nature that rises to the level of divine harmony, and thus the potential to be a perfectible (if not perfect) society, means that system has achieved both of its Paine-defined functions: it expresses the spirit of divine harmony, but is likewise simultaneously begotten from a nodal reform of war as system into society as system.

System, then, more so than any other term becomes a central one for Barlow in *The Columbiad.* Not twenty lines later, Barlow proclaims:

> Where system'd realms their mutual glories lend,
> And well-taught sires the cares of state attend,
> Thro every maze of man they learn to wind,
> Note each device that prompts the Proteus mind,
> What soft restraints the temper'd breast requires,
> To taste new joys and cherish new desires,
> Expand the selfish to the social flame,
> And rear the soul to deeds of nobler fame. (10:303–10)

The same lines that had been a function of the boundedness of *The Vision* are here subsumed into the idea of system, since what were previously mere "realms" are here "system'd realms." System is quite literally grounded; no longer the stuff of suns and seraphs, it is a defining feature of realms that mutually benefit each other in Barlow's new world order, but in a decided chiasmatic turn. While it is the individual human breast that must expand from selfish to social flame, it is precisely the "system'd realms" that nurture a society where the individual can possibly expand that flame. Rather than transcendent, the mind is systematized.

And since that selfish flame is not extinguished but simply rendered into the social and distributed into system, Barlow seems to have in mind Paine's own theory of rights, which posits that we have both natural and civil rights, and exchange the natural rights we cannot have the power to execute properly for the civil rights we share and trust the government to protect and execute.[30] Those exchanges are no less than nodes in this new system, places that update the health of the system. Collective rights thus hold equal sway with individual rights for Paine, and while there is little to no language of rights anywhere in either of Barlow's poems, it is nonetheless the case here that such "system'd realms" advocate and instantiate a reciprocal civil and individual responsibility, which, in its ability to "rear souls to nobler deeds," reads very much like a Barlowian version of Paine's view of the operation of rights in the political realm, creating a distinctive sociopolitical ethos that serves both democracy and its cosmopolitan ends.

Barlow's poetic rendering of system as a framework for his own understanding of rights and civic virtue suggests an axiomatic argument in regards to Barlow, Paine, and poetry. Barlow having adopted Paine's view of war as system, to an extent Paine's version of rights, and both war and rights' reciprocal functions as products of that system, then what is revealed beneath Barlow's "ideological unmasking" is system itself, a kind of trans-ideological reality that permeates the new cosmopolitan sensibility of the poem, if not the poem itself. If so, then it is perhaps neither as epic nor progress poem that *The Columbiad* should be considered, but rather as system. If, though, the tendency is always to "blame" system, then perhaps considering *The Columbiad*'s genre as system is not simply Paine's bequeathal to Barlow; it is likewise the reason for both their relative historical failures. Paine's reputation has been at best mixed; his "political legacy is today somewhat schizophrenic," and Barlow and his poetry's place in the canon of American Literature, early or otherwise, "does not initially seem to merit the effort to read it."[31] Barlow's claim that Paine was "one of the most instructive men I have known" returns to importance here—instructive certainly in certain thematic elements in his poems, but perhaps instructive too in how to survive the buffets of criticism and history to stand astride the political and literary tempests. In a study of Paine and poetry, it is fitting that the final words of *The Columbiad* stand as kind of terminal epigraph on that for which Paine and Barlow together can hope: "And all the joys, descending ages gain,/Repay thy labors and remove thy pain."

Notes

INTRODUCTION

1. Tennenhouse, *The Importance of Feeling English,* 2.
2. Philp, *Reforming Ideas in Britain,* 6.
3. Raven, "New Reading Histories, Print Culture, and the Identification of Change," 268.
4. John Katz, "The Age of Paine," *Wired Magazine,* May 1, 1995, www.wired.com /1995/05/paine/.
5. Francis Sherwood, *Vindication* (New York: W. W. Norton & Co., 2004), 148.

ONE. WIT IS NATURALLY A VOLUNTEER

1. James Playsted Woods calls it "one of the most important American magazines of the eighteenth century," and Lyon N. Richardson remarks, "Time and place conspired with the contributors to set the *Pennsylvania Magazine* high in importance among its eighteenth-century kin." Wood, *Magazines in the United States,* 15; Richardson, *A History of Early American Magazines,* 178.
2. Eric Foner, *Tom Paine and Revolutionary America* (New York: Oxford University Press, 2005), 19–20.
3. *Pennsylvania Packet, or The General Advertiser,* vol. IV, no. 161.
4. Fraistat's term appears prominently in two works: *The Poem and the Book: Interpreting Collections of Romantic Poetry* (Chapel Hill: University of North Carolina Press, 2012) and *Poems in Their Place: The Intertextuality and Order of Poetic Collections* (Chapel Hill: University of North Carolina Press, 2011).
5. Mark Parker, *Literary Magazines and British Romanticism* (Cambridge: Cambridge University Press, 2000), 3.
6. Larkin, *Thomas Paine and the Literature of Revolution,* 38–40.
7. Anne Ferry, *The Title to the Poem* (Stanford: Stanford University Press, 1996), 153.
8. Bennett, *Birth of the Museum,* 19.
9. Ibid., 25.

10. Woods, *Magazines in the Unites States*, 16. Woods also gives a full description of the title page.

11. Bennett, *Birth of the Museum*, 24.

12. Bennett contends that "culture, in this new logic, comprised a set of exercises through which those exposed to its influence were to be transformed into the active bearers and practitioners of the capacity for self-improvement that culture was held to embody." Paine's editing of the *Pennsylvania Magazine* substitutes "political independence" for self-improvement. Ibid., 24.

13. Castronuovo, "Poetry, Prose, and the Politics of Literary Form," 19.

14. Ibid., 21.

15. See especially Jack P. Greene, "An Uneasy Connection: An Analysis of the Preconditions of the American Revolution," in *Essays on the American Revolution*, eds. Stephen Kurtz and James Hutson (Chapel Hill: University of North Carolina Press, 1973): 32–80.

16. Castronuovo, "Poetry, Prose and the Politics of Literary Form," 25.

17. Bennett, *Birth of the Museum*, 97.

18. Thomas Paine, "The Utility of the Work Evinced," *Pennsylvania Magazine*, January 1775, 11.

19. Ibid., 11–12.

20. Brean Hammond, *Hackney for Bread: Professional Imaginative Writing in England, 1670–1740* (Oxford: Clarendon Press, 1997), 6.

21. Whale, *Imagination Under Pressure*, 45–46.

22. Ibid., 25.

23. See Patey, "The Institution of Criticism in the Eighteenth-Century," 3–31.

24. *Oxford English Dictionary Online*, s.v. "magic, n.," accessed April 1, 2017.

25. My argument echoes Edward Larkin's comment that writers at the magazine were "employing a strategy that enable[d] them to address the significant ideological issues of the revolutionary period allegorically. Insofar as it naturalized politics, by making it a part of the everyday, this strategy was designed to render politics more accessible to certain readers." *Thomas Paine and the Literature of Revolution*, 23.

26. Patey, "The Institution of Criticism in the Eighteenth-Century," 12; Fliegelman, *Declaring Independence*, 82.

27. Thomas Paine, "Reflections on the Life and Death of Lord Clive" *Pennsylvania Magazine*, March 1775, 108.

28. Fliegleman, *Declaring Independence*, 16. Fliegelman's point is about speaking and not printed text, but this is presented in the magazine as a spoken text.

29. Paine, "Reflections," 109.

30. Ibid., 110.

31. Ibid., 111.

32. "If Paine and the nameless poet are not the same, one wonders if there was any other literary Englishman in Philadelphia at that moment whose career and

feelings could have produced 'O, What a Pity!'" A. Owen Aldridge, *Thomas Paine's American Ideology* (Dover: University of Delaware Press, 1984), 289.

33. Larkin, *Thomas Paine and the Literature of Revolution*, 38.

34. Fliegelman, *Declaring Independence*, 40.

35. This kind of middle has become increasingly important in affect theory. Gregory J. Seigworth and Melissa Greg put it most succinctly: "Affect arises in the midst of *in-between-ness:* in the capacities to act and be acted upon." Gregory J. Seigworth and Melissa Gregg, eds., *The Affect Theory Reader* (Durham, NC: Duke University Press, 2010), 1.

36. Barnes, *States of Sympathy*, 31.

37. The phrase is Sandra Gustafson's, in *Eloquence of Power: Oratory and Performance in Early America* (Chapel Hill: University of North Carolina Press, 2000), xvi.

38. Barnes, *States of Sympathy*, 3.

39. Ibid., 3.

40. "No man was a warmer wisher for reconciliation than myself, before the fatal nineteenth of April 1775, but the moment the event of the day was made known, I rejected the hardened, sullen Pharaoh of England for ever." Paine, *Complete Writings*, 1:25.

41. Ahmed, *The Cultural Politics of Emotion*, 102.

42. Ibid., 103.

43. See William McCarthy, *Anna Letitia Barbauld: Voice of the Enlightenment* (Baltimore: Johns Hopkins University Press, 2008).

44. Robert Jones, "What Then Should Britons Feel? Anna Letitia Barbauld and the Plight of the Corsicans," *Women's Writing: The Elizabethan to Victorian Period* 9, no. 2 (2002): 285.

45. Thomas Paine, introduction to "Corsica," by Anna Letitia Barbauld, *Pennsylvania Magazine*, June 1775, 273.

46. Ibid.

47. Paine, in a letter to Henry Laurens, writes, "In the meantime, a person of this city desired me to give him some assistance in conducting a magazine, which I did without taking any bargain. . . . At the end of six months I thought it necessary to come to some contract." Paine, *Complete Writings*, 2:1160.

48. Richardson, *A History of Early American Magazines*, 193.

49. "Instances of English Longevity," *Pennsylvania Magazine*, February 1775, 59.

50. "A Remarkable Instance of AMERICAN LONGEVITY," *Pennsylvania Magazine*, May 1775, 220.

51. "A Remarkable Instance of American Increase," *Pennsylvania Magazine*, June 1775, 261.

52. "Instance of American Longevity," *Pennsylvania Magazine*, July 1775, 315.

53. "Substitutes for Tea," *Pennsylvania Magazine*, February 1775, 75.

54. Larkin, *Thomas Paine and the Literature of Revolution*, 37.

TWO. SPEAK OF IT AS IT IS

1. Aldridge, "Poetry of Thomas Paine," 81.

2. "Remarks," 488.

3. Arthur Schlesinger, "Liberty Tree: A Genealogy," *New England Quarterly* 25, no. 4 (1952): 437.

4. Taken from the entry on George Stevens in Thomas Campbell, *Specimens of the British Poets, with Biographical and Critical Notices, Vol. 6: Churchill, 1764, to Johnson, 1784* (London: Almond Murray, 1819), 436.

5. Paine, *Complete Writings*, 2:1091–92.

6. *Oxford English Dictionary Online*, s.v. "pledge, n.," accessed April 1, 2017.

7. Compare his claim in *Common Sense:* "'Tis not in numbers but unity that our great strength lies; yet our present numbers are sufficient to repel the force of all the world." Paine, *Complete Writings*, 1:31.

8. *Oxford English Dictionary Online*, s.v. "amain, adv.," accessed April 1, 2017.

9. Paine to Thomas Jefferson, May 1788, in *The Papers of Thomas Jefferson, Vol. 13: March 1788–October 1788*, ed. Julian P. Boyd (Princeton: Princeton University Press, 1956), 222–24.

10. *Oxford English Dictionary Online*, s.v. "flee, v.," accessed April 1, 2017.

11. Clark, *British Clubs and Societies 1580–1800*, ix.

12. Paine, *Complete Writings*, 2:1083–84.

13. "Remarks," 489.

14. Alan McNairn, *Behold the Hero: General Wolfe and the Arts in the Eighteenth Century* (Montreal and Kingston: McGill-Queeen's University Press, 1997), 87.

15. Clark, *British Clubs and Societies 1580–1800*, 6.

16. "Remarks," 490.

17. Roth, "Tom Paine and American Loneliness," 175.

18. "Most of our heroes, both ancient and modern, are celebrated in song of some kind or another; But as I know of none which pays that tribute to our immortal Wolfe, I herewith send you one. I have not pursued the worn out tract of modern song, but have thrown it into fable." Thomas Paine, introduction to "The Death of General Wolfe," *Pennsylvania Magazine*, March 1775, 134.

19. Annabel Patterson, *Fables of Power: Aesopian Writing and Political History* (Durham, NC: Duke University Press, 1991), 82.

20. Aldridge notes that "[Paine's] method derives from the method of Collins who, in his well-known odes 'Occasion'd by the Death of Mr. Thompson' and 'Written in the Beginning of the Year 1746' expressed grief by means of pictorial—not abstract—symbols." Aldridge, "The Poetry of Thomas Paine," 82.

21. Griffin, *Patriotism and Poetry*, 79. He is describing Thomson's take on "Britannia" here, and given Paine's later use of Thomson for his epigraph to *Common Sense* the connection seems logical.

22. "Remarks," 494.

23. Ibid.

24. The aural connection is found in many poems. *The Poetical Calendar By Francis Fawkes and William Woty* (London: J. Coote, 1763) for June 1763 includes "Inscription for the Monument of General Wolfe," the last stanza of which claims, "From the tempting vale he flew,/Heard his dying foe confess/In his death the honours due—/ Britons, if ye can—do less!" In *The Universal Melody* (London: J. Brown, 1766), "To the Memory of General Wolfe" includes these lines: "In the field alas, as in the state/The greatest merit meets the hardest fate // Streaming in blood, he rolls his livid eyes,/ And hearing shouts, has England lost, he cries/Oh no, I view the victors colours fly,/My country's conquered and in peace I die."

25. Some examples of these Wolfe poems include "Daphnis and Menalcas, A Pastoral Sacred to the Memory of the Late General James Wolfe" (London: Robert Dodsley, 1759); "The Encouraging General, A Song Sung by that True Gallant Gentlemen General Wolfe" in *Sadler's Wells Concerts* (London, 1760); "To the Memory of General Wolfe" in J. Copywell, *Shrubs of Parnassus* (London: J. Newberry, 1760); "Britannia's Tears: An Elegiac Ode Occasioned by the Death of General Wolfe" in Myles Cooper, *Poems on Several Occasions* (Oxford: W. Jackson, 1761); "A Poem Sacred to the Memory of General Wolfe" (New Haven: James Parker, 1760); "An Epitaph, Suitably Adapted to His Monument, Proposed to be in Westminster" in William Catton, *Poems on Several Occasions* (London, 1763); and "An Ode, Sacred to the Memory of General Wolfe" (London: J. Millan, 1759).

26. Griffin, *Patriotism and Poetry*, 79.

27. McNairn, *Behold the Hero*, 48.

28. Not surprisingly, Paine uses "induce" most often in his *Crisis* papers. See Manfred Putz and Jon K. Adams, *A Concordance to Thomas Paine's Common Sense and The American Crisis* (New York: Garland Publishing, 1989).

THREE. THE SHIFTED VISION

1. James Sambrook, introduction to Thomson, *Liberty*, 30–31. All quotes from Thomson's poetry are from Sambrook's edition.

2. Tennenhouse, *The Importance of Feeling English*, 1.

3. Gerrard, *The Patriot Opposition to Walpole*, 5.

4. Bailyn, "The Most Uncommon Pamphlet of the Revolution," 93.

5. Larkin, *Thomas Paine and the Literature of Revolution;* and Michael Everton, "The Would-be Author and the Real Bookseller: Thomas Paine and Eighteenth-Century Printing Ethics," *Early American Literature* 40, no. 1 (2005): 79–110. As with much of his work, Gimbel's *Thomas Paine: A Bibliographical Check List of Common Sense with an Account of Its Publication* is not simply the best retelling of the events surrounding the publication of Paine's pamphlet; it is also the most thorough check list of *Common Sense*'s various editions and issues. See also Thomas Adams, *The American Controversy: A Bibliographical Study of the British Pamphlets about the American Disputes, 1764–1783* (Providence: Brown University Press, 1980).

6. Gimbel, *Bibliographical Check List,* 34.

7. Ibid., 46. In his letter to Henry Laurens dated January 14,1779, Paine recounts, "I then enlarged the pamphlet . . . , printed 6,000 at my own expense, 3,000 by B. Towne, 3,000 by Styner & Cist, and delivered them ready stitched and fit for sale to Mr. Bradford at the Coffee-house." Paine, *Complete Writings,* 2:1162.

8. Adams, "The Authorship and Printing of *Plain Truth* by 'Candidus,'" 234; Larkin, *Thomas Paine and the Literature of Revolution,* 54.

9. Paine to Laurens, January 14, 1779, in *Complete Writings,* 2:1163.

10. Genette, *Paratexts,* 2.

11. *Oxford English Dictionary Online,* s.v. "licence, n.," def. 3b, accessed April 1, 2017.

12. Genette says "Whatever aesthetic or ideological investment the author makes in a paratextual element, . . . whatever coquettishness or paradoxical reversal he puts into it, the paratextual element is always subordinate to 'its' text, and this functionality determines the essence of its appeal and its existence." *Paratexts,* 12.

13. *Oxford English Dictionary,* s.v. "ordain, v.," defs. 1 and 2, accessed April 1, 2017.

14. *Oxford English Dictionary,* s.v. "shift, n.," def. 3a, accessed April 01, 2017.

15. Kramnick, "An Aesthetics and Ecology of Presence," 321.

16. Terry, "Thomson and the Druids," 142.

17. Ibid., 153.

18. Paine, *Complete Writings,* 1:3.

19. Ibid., 4–6.

20. This is certainly a variation of what has been called the state as a work of art. See Eric Slauter's *The State as a Work of Art: The Cultural Origins of the Constitution* (Chicago: University of Chicago Press, 2009), in which Paine plays a prominent early role.

21. Dix, "James Thomson and the Progress of the Progress Poem," 118; Griffith, "The Progress Pieces of the Eighteenth-Century, with a Check-list," 218, 225.

22. Paine, *Complete Writings,* 1:5.

23. While Paine in a sense creates a *translatio democracii* to replace the *translatio imperii,* I would suggest that the other half of the progress poem, the *translatio artis,* is embedded within in the communal interchange Paine describes.

24. Paine, *Complete Writings,* 1:6.

25. Kramnick, "An Aesthetics and Ecology of Presence," 315.

26. Paine, *Complete Writings,* 1:17.

27. Roth, "Tom Paine and American Loneliness," 175.

28. Hoffman, "Paine and Prejudice," 393.

29. Paine, *Complete Writings,* 1:17.

30. Loughran, *The Republic in Print,* 73.

31. Kramnick, "An Aesthetics and Ecology of Presence," 325.

32. Rombes, "Speculative Discourses," 84.

33. Fulford, "Britannia's Heart of Oak," 193.

34. Michael P. Kramer, *Imagining Language in America: From the Revolution to the Civil War* (Princeton: Princeton University Press, 1992), 45.

35. More, *Strictures, Critical and Sentimental, on Thomson's Seasons,* 194.

36. Loughran, *The Republic in Print,* 75–77.

37. Patricia Meyer Spacks, *Reading Eighteenth-Century Poetry* (London: Wiley-Blackwell, 2009), 44.

38. Ibid., 47; Jung, "Image Making in James Thomson's *The Seasons,*" 584.

39. Loughran, *The Republic in Print,* 75.

40. See Gregory Claeys, *Thomas Paine: Social and Political Thought* (New York: Routledge, 1989), 45–51.

41. Griffin, *Patriotism and Poetry,* 82–83.

42. Paine, *Complete Writings,* 1:39.

43. The definitions were found together for the first time in the famous fourth edition of Johnson's dictionary in 1773.

44. Gerrard, *The Patriot Opposition to Walpole,* 6

45. Suvir Kaul, *Poems of Nation, Anthems of Empire* (Charlottesville, University of Virginia Press, 2000), 176.

46. Tennenhouse, *The Importance of Feeling English,* 2.

47. Loughran, *The Republic in Print,* 77.

FOUR. PEN AND SOUL; GLORY AND NOTHING

1. Bertelsen, *The Nonsense Club,* 118.

2. Philip Foner, introduction to *The Complete Writings of Thomas Paine,* vol. 1 (New York: Citadel Press, 1945), xvi.

3. Neil York, "George III, Tyrant," 435, 457.

4. *The Crisis,* no. 1, January 20, 1775 (London: T. W. Shaw).

5. Paine, *Complete Writings,* 1:58.

6. Warner, *The Letters of the Republic,* xi.

7. *The Crisis,* no. 24, July 1, 1775 (London: T. W. Shaw).

8. Ibid.

9. Ibid.

10. *North Briton,* no. 37, February 12, 1763.

11. Ibid.

12. All quotations of Churchill's poetry are taken from *The Poetical Works of Charles Churchill,* edited by Douglas Grant.

13. Bertelsen, *The Nonsense Club,* 117

14. Golden, "Sterility and Eminence," 33.

15. Brewer, "The Tactility of Authorial Names," 195.

16. *Oxford English Dictionary,* s.v. "controlment, n.," accessed April 1, 2017.

17. Bertelsen, *The Nonsense Club,* 128.

18. Ibid., 117.

19. Golden, "Sterility and Eminence," 334.

20. Howe had issued similar proclamations on July 14 and September 19 of 1776.

21. Paine, *Complete Writings*, 1:59. Paine says something similar in his sixth *Letter to the Citizens of the United States*: "John Adams and Timothy Pickering were men whom nothing but the accidents of the times rendered visible on the political horizon." *Complete Writings*, 2:936.

22. James Ferguson, *An Easy Introduction to Astronomy, for Young Gentlemen and Ladies*, 2nd ed.(London: T. Cadell, 1764), 111. Ferguson goes on the describe the horizon as that "which limits our view" at least three more times in the section of his *Easy Introduction* entitled "On the Method of Finding the LATITUDES and LONGITUDES of Places." Paine's use of "antipodes" seems likewise drawn from Ferguson in that section.

23. Briggs, "The Brain, Too Finely Wrought," 40.

24. Paine, *Complete Writings*, 1:59.

25. John Milton, *Paradise Lost*, in *The Poetical Works of John Milton*, vol. 1, ed. Helen Darbishire (Oxford: Oxford University Press, 1963).

26. Vickers, *My Pen and My Soul*, 41.

27. Paine, *Complete Writings, CW*, 1:59.

28. Ibid., 1:63.

29. Ibid.,1:67

30. Ibid., 1:68.

31. Briggs, "The Brain, Too Finely Wrought," 39.

32. Loughran, *The Republic in Print*, 72

33. Paine, *Complete Writings*, 1:59.

34. Johnson has eleven separate definitions for "nature," including "The native state or properties of anything, by which it is discriminated from other things" (def. 2) and "Disposition of mind; temper" (def. 4). Samuel Johnson, *A Dictionary of the English Language: A Digital Edition of the 1755 Classic by Samuel Johnson*, s.v. "Nature," ed. Brandi Besalke, http://johnsonsdictionaryonline.com/?p=15301, last modified June 26, 2013.

35. See Aldridge, "The Poetry of Thomas Paine," for a description of a poem that has come to be called "An Address to Lord Howe" but was initially addressed to George III.

36. Paine, *Complete Writings*, 1:63.

37. Ibid., 1:72.

38. Brewer, "The Tactility of Authorial Names," 196. While Brewer argues that such use of the authorial name evacuates such marks of any real personality, Paine leverages it for the exact opposite reason.

39. William Warner suggests another important valence of the meaning of crisis for Paine, as it "indexes a period of political emergency, suspenseful struggle, fluid

events and impending decision." Each of these meanings is embedded in Paine's presentation of self here. William Warner, *Protocols of Liberty: Communication Innovation and the American Revolution* (Chicago: University of Chicago Press, 2013), 3.

40. Paine, *Complete Writings*, 1:72.

41. Nancy Ruttenberg. *Democratic Personality: Popular Voice and the Trial of American Authorship* (Stanford: Stanford University Press, 1998), 4.

FIVE. THE FIELD OF IMAGINATION

1. Paine, *Complete Writings*, 1:475.

2. In a scheme suggested by David Hoffman concerning Paine's "testimonial strategies," this makes the poet-prophets "unreliable witnesses." Hoffman, "Cross-Examining Scripture."

3. Paine, *Complete Writings*, 1:475. Perhaps surprisingly, Paine seems to have had Bishop Robert Lowth in mind when he wrote these lines. As Lowth opines, "The Hebrew poetry has likewise another property altogether peculiar to metrical composition. Writers who are confined within the trammels of verse, are generally indulged with the license of using words in a sense and manner remote from their common acceptation, and in some degree contrary to the analogy of language, so that sometimes they shorten them by taking from the number of the syllables, and sometimes venture to add a syllable for the sake of adapting them to their immediate purpose." Robert Lowth, *Lectures on the Sacred Poetry of the Hebrews* (London: J. Johnson, 1787), 58.

4. Paine, *Complete Writings*, 1:475.

5. Paine, *Complete Writings*, 1:496.

6. Whale, *Imagination Under Pressure*, 1.

7. Paine, *Complete Writings*, 2:214.

8. Ibid. 2:254.

9. Ibid. 2:843.

10. Ibid. 2:844.

11. Ibid.

12. Whale, *Imagination Under Pressure*, 42.

13. "Confronted with the chaos of political crisis or the variety of the artistic text, Paine deploys this analogy of the straight line. It can be conveniently used to connect his belief in geometry with his belief in individualism; it can be made to fit the universal laws of nature and with the individual intervention on behalf of social enlightenment." Ibid., 59.

14. *Oxford English Dictionary*, s.v. "bent, n. 2," def. 1a, accessed April 1, 2017.

15. Whale notes, "Precisely because of [imagination's] power, emphasis is placed on its containment by judgement. There is a clash of source and direction." Within the curvature of his bent towards science, that clash is reconciled. *Imagination Under Pressure*, 45.

16. *Oxford English Dictionary,* s.v. "turn, n.," accessed April 1, 2017. See especially def. 1.

17. *Oxford English Dictionary,* s.v. "bent, n. 1," def. 5a, accessed April 1, 2017.

18. See Harold Love, *The Culture and Commerce of Texts: Scribal Publication in Seventeenth-Century England* (Boston: University of Massachusetts Press, 1998); Melanie Bigold, *Women of Letters, Manuscript Circulation, and Print Afterlives in the Eighteenth Century* (London: Palgrave MacMillan, 2013); and David McKitterick, *Print, Manuscript, and the Search for Order, 1450–1830* (Cambridge: Cambridge University Press, 2003) for a small sampling of the scholarship on the porous print/manuscript divide in the eighteenth century.

19. Philp, *Reforming Ideas in Britain,* 6.

20. Paine's letter to Kitty Nicholson Few reveals him as wonderfully sensitive and thoughtful on the subject of marriage. If these lyrical poems have epistolary parallels, this letter is the most important one. Paine to Kitty Nicholson Few, in *Complete Writings,* 2:1274–78.

21. David Freeman Hawke notes that Smyth was "an English banker whose sympathy for the French Revolution had several years ago brought friendship with Paine." David Freeman Hawke, *Paine* (New York: Harper and Rowe, 1974), 317.

22. Henry Yorke relates that Paine "amused himself with carrying on an epistolary correspondence with Lady S**** under the assumed name of 'The Castle in the Air' and her Ladyship answered, under the title of 'The Little Corner of the World;' which has been continued to the present without intermission." Henry Yorke, *Letters from France, 1802,* 2 vols. (London: H.Y. Symonds, 1804), 2:346.

23. Stewart, *Poetry and the Fate of the Senses,* 46.

24. Ibid.

25. "I do not mean by this declaration to condemn those who believe otherwise; they have the same right to their belief as I have to mine. But it is necessary to the happiness of man that he be mentally faithful to himself. Infidelity does not consist in believing, or in disbelieving; it consists in professing to believe what he does not believe." Paine, *Complete Writings,*1:464.

26. Ibid.

27. "What is Love?" AMS to Robert Smith, Colonel Richard Gimbel Collection of Thomas Paine Papers, B P165, series I, American Philosophical Society.

28. Jacques Derrida, *Speech and Phenomena: And Other Essays on Husserl's Theory of Signs,* trans. David Allison (Evanston: Northwestern University Press, 1973), 156.

29. Here stands a poetically ideal embodiment of Foucault's description of penal changes in the late eighteenth century: "Punishment then, will tend to become the most hidden part of the penal process. This has several consequences: it leaves the domain of the more or less everyday perception and enters that of the abstract consciousness, its effectiveness is seen as resulting from its inevitability, not from its visible intensity." *Discipline and Punish,* 9.

SIX. TOM THE BODICE-MAKER

1. See Linda Colley, *Britons: Forging the Nation 1707–1837* (New Haven: Yale University Press, 1992) and Benedict Anderson, *Imagined Communities: Reflections on the Origin and Spread of Nationalism*, rev. ed. (New York: Verso, 2016).

2. Kevin Gilmartin, *Print Politics: The Press and Radical Opposition in Early Nineteenth-Century England* (Cambridge: Cambridge University Press, 1996), 5.

3. *John Bull Roused from his Lethargy*, printed by C. L. Hannsell, Hosier Lane. The rumors of Paine's penchant for alcohol are unfortunately an inseparable part of the biographies that were peddled in the 1790s. The most well known was by Francis Oldys, pseudonym of George Chalmers, whose *Life of Thomas Paine* (1794) was sponsored by the British government in an attempt to publicly discredit Paine.

4. Or, as the similarity of bullocks to bollocks hints, his testicles as well.

5. Foucault, *Discipline and Punish*, 11.

6. *The British Lyon Rous'd; Or, John Bull For Ever*, London, n.d.

7. As Ian Haywood notes, "The demonization of Paine and the suppression of his works played into the hands of radical 'martyrology.'" Haywood is writing largely about prints and caricature, but these 1790s poems form the vanguard of that radical demonization. Ian Heywood, *Romanticism and Caricature* (Cambridge: Cambridge University Press, 2013), 112.

8. Samuel Ashby, *Miscellaneous Poems*, London: W. Miller, 1794.

9. *Oxford English Dictionary*, s.v. "Christmas-box, n.," accessed April 1, 2017.

10. "Common Sense; or, An Antidote Against Paine" from *Gower's Patriotic Songster*, remarks, "What think you, brave Britons, of freedom like this? / 'Tis highly approv'd by Tom Paine" (49–50).

11. Samuel Johnson, *A Dictionary of the English Language: A Digital Edition of the 1755 Classic by Samuel Johnson*, s.v. "Cajole," ed. Brandi Besalke, http://johnsonsdictionaryonline.com/?page_id=7070&i=314, last modified June 26, 2013.

12. The broadside *Mighty Tom Paine* claims that "In America's War, 'tis well known his endeavour, / To blow up the Flame that between us began; / And he strain'd ev'ry nerve for to part us forever" (9–11). While Paine is not feminized in this poem, here too he is depicted as feeling not just excessively but nervously.

13. *Mighty Tom Paine* again provides a vital echo: "He talks of Equality one with another, / As if such a thing would be possibly done; / Wou'd make us all equal like Sister and Brother, / Forgetting the diff'rence 'twixt Father and Son" (17–20). There, too, Paine's attempts at levelling hierarchical relationships render them as unnatural perversions.

14. John Jackson's poem "Burning of Tom Paine in Effigy" boasts "Let Paine, with false pity, the destiny mock / Of a Monarch whose head he has help'd to the block." John Jackson, *Poems on Several Occasions* (London: J. Bell, 1797), 17–18.

15. As "Pat-Riot" from *Gower's Patriotic Songster* suggests, "I dare not be *loyal*, for this *loyal* reason—/ My *tutor*, Tom Paine, tells me loyalty's *treason*" (9–10). A number of other poems cast Paine as a teacher of illicit morals and ideas.

16. The quote is from Shirley Samuels, "Infidelity and Contagion: The Rhetoric of Revolution," *Early American Literature* 22, no. 2 (Fall 1987): 188. Samuels is writing in context about a Timothy Dwight discourse, but those concerns about the sexual proclivities of Paine's democratic, populist leanings are nearly identical.

17. A number of poems seek to relate Paine to fish. An American poem, Geoffrey Touchstone's *He Wou'd Be a Poet, or Nature will be Nature Still* (Philadelphia, 1796) notes that "The loaves and fishes, seem to be his care,/ Let Him divide—and trust him for his share,/ Or else his system, of the Rights of Man,/ Is all a Bug-bear, and a take in, plan" (232–35). Two interesting poems, *Casino: A Mock Heroic Poem* (London: J. Bell, 1793) and its response, *Putt: A Mock Heroic Poem* (Southampton: T. Skelton, 1793), frame Paine's political views as rules in competing card games. Casino proclaims, "Long reign with Whist and Cribbage, Hand in Hand:/ And may, in spite of frantic Paine's Endeavour,/ Great George and great Casino live forever" (141–43). Putt, while saying "Not Whist I dare to sing" (3), describes the play of King and Queen cards in putt thus: "May these together never act in vain,/ and dare the threats of Priestly and of Paine" (115–16). The poem's fictional narrator is, simply, "A Fisherman."

18. *Oxford English Dictionary*, s.v. "havoc, n.," accessed April 1, 2017.

19. Klancher, *The Making of English Reading Audiences*, 99.

20. The Gordon Riots were the preeminent form of social violence that threatened to destabilize the existing social order of late eighteenth-century Britain. See Christopher Hibbert, *King Mob* (London: Longmans, Green, & Co., 1958), and Nicholas Rogers, *Crowds, Culture, and Politics in Georgian Britain* (Oxford: Clarendon Press, 1998).

21. *Oxford English Dictionary*, s.v. "squeeze, n.," accessed April 1, 2017.

22. Jonathan Couch describes the elleck, or cur fish, thus: "The Elleck is caught on the west coast of England and Ireland at all seasons; and it is known also at the extremity of Scotland; where, however, as I learn from C.W. Peach, Esq., of Wick, it is in such little esteem as food, as for the most part to be thrown aside as worthless." Jonathan Couch, *A History of the Fishes of the British Isles*, vol. 2 (London: Groombridge and Sons, 1863), 19.

23. *Oxford English Dictionary*, s.v. "rhapsody, n.," def. 2a, accessed April 1, 2017.

SEVEN. THE MANLY PAGE

1. In an otherwise insightful article, Béranger mentions Freneau's writings about Paine twice but never calls him one of Freneau's heroes.

2. Wertheimer, "Commencement Ceremonies," 35.

3. *Oxford English Dictionary*, s.v. "sway, n.," accessed April 1, 2017.

4. Paine, *Complete Writings*, 1:6.

5. Ibid., 1:29.

6. Castronuovo, "Poetry, Prose, and the Politics of Literary Form," 21.

7. Philip Freneua, "A Poetical Address to the People of the United States," *National Gazette,* October 31, 1791.

8. Freneau published a number of his poems in newspapers first, especially those he edited himself. See Judith Hiltner, *The Newspaper Verse of Philip Freneau: An Edition and Bibliographical Survey* (Troy, NY: Whitson Publishing, 1986).

9. *Oxford English Dictionary,* s.v. "strange, adj.," accessed April 1, 2017.

10. Vitzthum, *Land and Sea,* 162.

11. Blakemore, *Literature, Intertextuality, and the American Revolution,* 51.

12. Ibid., 62.

13. One may also wish to read Paine's drawing forth of "reforms" from "reason's source" as a kind of generation that sidesteps the same male/female binary.

14. Vitzthum, *Land and Sea,* 14.

15. Paine, *Complete Writings,* 1:275–76.

16. Ibid., 1:497.

17. Freneau to Dr. J. W. Francis, May 15, 1815, courtesy of the Monmouth County Historical Association.

18. Paine, *Complete Writings,* 1:481.

EIGHT. REPAY THY LABORS

1. Table of contents for collected works, Joel Barlow papers, 1775–1935, MS Am 1448(60), Houghton Library, Harvard University.

2. The letter appeared in the *Belfast Monthly Magazine* 7, no. 37 (Aug 31, 1811): 90–93. It also appeared in Charles Burr Todd's biography, *Life and Letters of Joel Barlow, LL.D.: Poet, Statesman, Philosopher* (New York: G.P. Putnam & Sons, 1886), but never, as Barlow intended, in any edition of his own works.

3. "It has been intimated to me, by a gentleman who has favored me with his correspondence on the subject of the work (*Age of Reason*) whose name I am not at liberty to mention, that Paine's deistical productions do not form in him *a distinctive character.*" Cheetham, *The Life of Thomas Paine,* 93.

4. Paine, *Complete Writings,* 1:5.

5. Ibid.

6. Robert Lamb notes Paine's preoccupation with human nature as a function of his views on "political socialisation." Lamb, *Thomas Paine and Human Rights,* 75.

7. "Can these be fashion'd on the social plan,/ Or boast a lineage with the race of man?" (2:41–42); "While milder arts, with social joys refined/ Inspire new beauties in the growing mind" (2:159–60); "If human souls for social compact given,/ Inform their nature with the stamp of heaven,/ Why the dread gloom forever must they rove?" (2:227–28); "No social joys their wayward passions prove;/ Nor peace, nor pleasure treads the savage grove" (2:579–80); "But nobler joys his righteous laws

impart; To aid the life and mould the social heart" (3:377–78); "Drives fraud and rapine from their nightly spoil,/And social nature wakes to peaceful toil" (4:49–50); "While the dark tribes in social aid combine,/Exchange their treasures and their joys refine" (4:427–28); "Shed the bright beams of knowledge on the mind,/For social compact harmonize mankind" (7:159–60); "When different tribes, in social bands combined,/Their local views the joyless soul confined." (8:65–66).

8. Sambrook, *James Thomson*, 145.

9. Barlow's journals contain several references to Thomson. His diary on travels to Havre and New York notes, "On Richmond Hill, we have a prospect of the country for about a dozen miles in circuit which is far more magnificent and enchanting than one can conceive from Thomson's description of it in his Summer." Diary, 25 May–12 September [1788], Joel Barlow papers, 1775–1935, MS Am 1448(9), Houghton Library, Harvard University.

10. Dowling, *Poetry and Ideology*, 20.

11. *Oxford English Dictionary*, s.v. "enlarge, v.," def. 3b, and "extend, v." def. 3b, 5b, and 11a, accessed April 1, 2017.

12. *Oxford English Dictionary*, s.v. "ascend, v.," def. 3, accessed April 1, 2017.

13. Paine, *Complete Writings*, 2:242.

14. "[Paine's] view is that the state functions to promote our happiness in a chiefly *negative* sense." Lamb, *Thomas Paine and the Idea of Human Rights*, 74.

15. Paine, *Complete Writings*, 2:240.

16. "Democratic mind" is Lamb's term for "the belief that individuals go through some kind of ideational transformation as they are included in the democratic process." For Barlow, it is cosmopolitanism that activates the same mind. Lamb, *Thomas Paine and the Idea of Human Rights*, 75.

17. Ibid., 105.

18. Barlow makes this explicit in *The Columbiad* with his engraved plates included in the 1807 edition. The final one was titled "The Final Resignation of the Prejudices." See Steven Blakemore, *Joel Barlow's Columbiad*, 17, 140.

19. John P. McWilliams, Jr., *The American Epic: Transforming a Genre, 1770–1860*, Cambridge: Cambridge University Press, 1989, 4.

20. In his 1803 notebook, Barlow quotes "Thomson on Public Charity" and copies lines from book 4 of "Liberty." He also included a note below the quotation: "Thomson's Virtues; Genii of England: are courage, charity, justice, sincerity, philosophy, retirement, independence, modesty, labour, imagination, and religion." Notebook, 1802, Joel Barlow papers, 1775–1935, MS Am 1448(17), Houghton Library, Harvard University.

21. Dowling, *Poetry and Ideology*, 4.

22. See the 1809 edition of *The Coumbiad*, viii; Dowling, *Poetry and Ideology*, 58.

23. Dowling, *Poetry and Ideology*, 58.

24. Paine, *Complete Writings*, 1:285.

25. Ibid., 1:343.

26. Ibid.

27. Lamb, *Thomas Paine and the Idea of Human Rights,* 170.

28. Kevin Kelly, *Out of Control: The New Biology of Machines, Social Systems, and the Economic World* (Cambridge, MA: Perseus Books, 1994), 122.

29. Paine, *Complete Writings,* 1:343.

30. Ibid., 1:275–76.

31. Lamb, *Thomas Paine and the Idea of Human Rights,* 1–2; Blakemore, *Joel Barlow's Columbiad,* 3.

Bibliography

Adams, Thomas. "The Authorship and Printing of *Plain Truth* by 'Candidus.'" *Papers of the Bibliographical Society of America* 49, no. 3 (1955): 230–48.

Aldridge, A. Owen. "The Poetry of Thomas Paine." *Pennsylvania Magazine of History and Biography* 79, no. 1 (1955): 81–99.

Bailyn, Bernard. "The Most Uncommon Pamphlet of the Revolution: *Common Sense*." *American Heritage* 25, no. 1 (1973): 36–41, 91–93.

Barnes, Elizabeth. *States of Sympathy: Seduction and Democracy in the American Novel.* New York: Columbia University Press, 1997.

Barlow, Joel. *The Works of Joel Barlow in Two Volumes.* New York: Scholars Facsimiles Reprints, 1970.

Bennettt, Tony. *The Birth of the Museum: History, Theory, Politics.* London: Routledge, 1995.

Béranger, Jean. "Héroïsation et révolution dans la poésie de Freneau." *Revue française d'études américaines* 14, no. 40 (1989): 161–74.

Bertelsen, Lance. *The Nonsense Club: Literature and Popular Culture, 1749–1764.* Oxford: Clarendon Press, 1985.

Blakemore, Steven. *Joel Barlow's "Columbiad": A Bicentenntial Reading.* Knoxville: University of Tennessee Press, 2007.

———. *Literature, Intertextuality, and the American Revolution: From Common Sense to Rip Van Winkle.* Latham, MD: Fairleigh Dickinson University Press, 2014.

Brewer, David. "The Tactility of Authorial Names." *The Eighteenth-Century* 54, no. 2 (2013): 195–213.

Briggs, Peter M. "'The Brain, Too Finely Wrought.'" *Modern Language Studies* 14, no. 4 (Autumn 1984): 39–53.

Castronovo, Russ. "Poetry, Prose, and the Politics of Literary Form." In *A Companion to American Literary Studies,* edited by Caroline Levander and Robert Levine, 15–28. London: Wiley Blackwell, 2011.

Cheetham, James. *The Life of Thomas Paine.* London: A. Maxwell, 1817.

Choice Spirit's Chaplet, The; or, A Poesy from Parnassus. Compiled by George Alexander Stevens. London: John Dunn, 1771.

Choice Selection of Civic Songs, A. London, 1795.

Churchill, Charles. *The Poetical Works of Charles Churchill.* Edited by Douglas Grant. Oxford: Clarendon Press, 1956.

Clark, Peter. *British Clubs and Societies, 1580–1800: The Origins of an Associational World.* Oxford: Clarendon Press, 2000.

Dix, Robin. "James Thomson and the Progress of the Progress Poem: From *Liberty* to *The Castle of Indolence.*" In *James Thomson: Essays for the Tercentenary,* edited by Richard Terry, 117–41. Liverpool: Liverpool University Press, 2000.

Dowling, William. *Poetry and Ideology in Revolutionary Connecticut.* Athens: University of Georgia Press, 1990.

Fliegelman, Jay. *Declaring Independence: Jefferson, Natural Language, and the Culture of Performance.* Stanford: Stanford University Press, 1993.

Foucault, Michel. *Discipline and Punish: The Birth of the Prison.* Translated by Alan Sheridan. New York: Vintage Books, 1977.

Freneau, Philip. *The Poems of Philip Freneau.* Edited by Fred Lewis Pattee. 3 vols. Princeton: Princeton Historical Society, 1902.

Fulford, Tim. "Britannia's Heart of Oak: Thomson, Garrick, and the Language of Eighteenth-Century Patriotism." In *James Thomson: Essays for the Tercentenary,* edited by Richard Terry, 191–215. Liverpool: Liverpool University Press, 2000.

Gerrard, Christine. *The Patriot Opposition to Walpole: Politics, Poetry, and Myth, 1725–1742.* Oxford: Clarendon Press, 1995.

Genette, Gerard. *Paratexts: Thresholds of Interpretation.* Translated by Jane Lewen. Cambridge: Cambridge University Press, 1997.

Gimbel, Richard. *Thomas Paine: A Bibliographical Check List of Common Sense with an Account of Its Publication.* New Haven: Yale University Press, 1956.

Golden, Morris. "Sterility and Eminence in the Poetry of Charles Churchill." *Journal of English and German Philology* 66, no. 3 (July 1967): 333–46.

Gower's Patriotic Songster; or, Loyalist's Vocal Companion. Kidderminster: G. Gower, 1794.

Griffin, Dustin. *Patriotism and Poetry in Eighteenth-Century Britain.* Cambridge: Cambridge University Press, 2002.

Griffith, R. H. "The Progress Pieces of the Eighteenth-Century, with a Check-List." *Texas Review* 5, no. 3 (April 1920): 218–34.

Hoffman, David. "Cross-Examining Scripture: Testimonial Strategies in Thomas Paine's *The Age of Reason.*" *Rhetorica: A Journal of the History of Rhetoric* 31, no. 3 (Summer 2013): 261–95.

———. "Paine and Prejudice: Rhetorical Leadership through Perceptual Framing in *Common Sense.*" *Rhetoric and Public Affairs* 9, no. 3 (2006): 373–410.

Jones, Robert. "What Then Should Britons Feel? Anna Letitia Barbauld and the Plight of the Corsicans." *Women's Writing: The Elizabethan to Victorian Period* 9, no. 2 (2002): 285–303.

Jung, Sandro. "Image Making in James Thomson's *The Seasons*." *SEL* 53, no. 3 (Summer 2013): 583–99.

Klancher, Jon. *The Making of English Reading Audiences, 1790–1832*. Madison: University of Wisconsin Press, 1987.

Kramnick, Jonathan. "An Aesthetics and Ecology of Presence." *European Romantic Review* 26, no. 3 (2015): 315–27.

Lamb, Robert. *Thomas Paine and the Idea of Human Rights*. Cambridge: Cambridge University Press, 2015.

Larkin, Edward. *Thomas Paine and the Literature of Revolution*. Cambridge: Cambridge University Press, 2006.

Loughran, Tricia. *The Republic in Print: Print Culture in the Age of U.S. Nation Building, 1770–1870*. New York: Columbia University Press, 2007.

Lowth, Robert. *Lectures on the Sacred Poetry of the Hebrews*. London: J. Johnson, 1787.

Mighty Tom Paine. Hull[?], 1795[?].

More, John. *Strictures, Critical and Sentimental, on Thomson's Seasons*. London: Richardson Urquhart, 1777.

Mott, Frank. *History of the American Magazine*. 5 vols. Cambridge: Harvard Belknap Press, 1934.

North Briton. 2 vols. London: J. Williams, 1763.

Paine, Thomas. *The Complete Writings of Thomas Paine*. Edited by Philip Foner. 2 vols. New York: Citadel Press, 1945.

———. *The Works of Thomas Paine*. 2 vols. Philadelphia: James Carey, 1797.

———. *The Writings of Thomas Paine*. Edited by Moncure Conway. 4 vols. New York: G. P. Putnam and Sons, 1894.

Patey, Douglas. "The Institution of Criticism in the Eighteenth-Century." In *The Cambridge History of Literary Criticism*, edited by H. B Nisbet and Claude Rawson, 3–32. Cambridge: Cambridge University Press, 1997.

Pennsylvania Magazine, or American Monthly Museum. Philadelphia: Robert Aitken, 1775.

Philp, Mark. *Reforming Ideas in Britain: Politics and Language in the Shadow of the French Revolution, 1789–1815*. Cambridge: Cambridge University Press, 2014.

Pindar, Peter [John Walcott]. *The Complete Works of Peter Pindar*. 3 Vols. London: John Walker, 1794.

Raven, James. "New Reading Histories, Print Culture, and the Identification of Change: The Case of Eighteenth-Century England." *Social History* 23, no. 3 (October 1998): 268–87.

"Remarks on the Pretensions of Thomas Paine, Author of 'Common Sense,' to The Character of a Poet." *Port Folio*, 3rd ser., vol. 6, no. 5 (1815): 488–97.

Richardson, Lyon N. *A History of Early American Magazines, 1741–1789*. Octagon Books, New York: 1978.

Rombes, Nicholas. "Speculative Discourses: Uses of the Future in the Declaration, *The Federalist Papers*, Jefferson, and Paine." In *Making America/Making American*

Literature: Franklin to Cooper, edited by Robert Lee and W. M. Verhoeven, 77–92. Amsterdam: Rodopi, 1995.

Roth, Martin. "Tom Paine and American Loneliness." *Early American Literature* 22, no. 2 (Fall 1987): 175–82.

Sambrook, James. *James Thomson, 1700–1748: A Life.* Oxford: Clarendon Press, 1991.

Shirley Samuels. "Infidelity and Contagion: The Rhetoric of Revolution." *Early American Literature* 22, no. 2 (Fall 1987): 183–91.

Schlesinger, Arthur. "Liberty Tree: A Genealogy." *New England Quarterly* 25, no. 4 (1952): 435–58.

Stewart, Susan. *Poetry and the Fate of the Senses.* Chicago: University of Chicago Press, 2002.

Tennenhouse, Leonard. *The Importance of Feeling English: American Literature and the British Diaspora, 1750–1850.* Princeton: Princeton University Press, 2007.

Terry, Richard. "Thomson and the Druids." In *James Thomson: Essays for the Tercentenary,* edited by Richard Terry, 141–65. Liverpool: Liverpool University Press, 2000.

Thomson, James. *Liberty, The Castle of Indolence, and Other Poems.* Edited by James Sambrook. Oxford: Clarendon Press, 1986.

Tribute to Liberty, A; or, A Collection of Select Songs. London, 1793.

Vickers, Vikki J. *"My Pen and My Soul Have Ever Gone Together": Thomas Paine and the American Revolution.* New York: Routledge, 2006

Vitzthum, Richard. *Land and Sea: The Lyrical Poetry of Philip Freneau.* Minneapolis: University of Minnesota Press, 1978.

Warner, Michael. *The Letters of the Republic: Publication and the Public Sphere in Eighteenth-Century America.* Cambridge: Harvard University Press, 1990.

Wertheimer, Eric. "Commencement Ceremonies: History and Identity in 'The Rising Glory of America,' 1771 and 1786." *Early American Literature* 29, no. 1 (1994): 35.

Whale, John. *Imagination Under Pressure, 1789–1832: Aesthetics, Politics, Utility.* Cambridge: Cambridge University Press, 2000.

Woods, James Playsted. *Magazines in the Unites States.* 3rd ed. New York: Ronald Press Company, 1971.

York, Neil. "George III, Tyrant: The *Crisis* as Critic of Empire, 1775–1776." *History* 94, no. 4 (October 2009): 434–60.

Index